AUDREY ELLIS

Audrey Ellis has written more than forty practical and imaginative cookery books. Well known as a cookery demonstrator and broadcaster, she contributes regularly to several national magazines and acts as food adviser to television programmes. Mrs Ellis, who is also a member of the Association of Home Economists, travels widely but manages to combine all these activities with looking after a home and family.

HINTS
FOR
MODERN
COOKS

AUDREY ELLIS

Hamlyn Paperbacks

HINTS FOR MODERN COOKS

isbn 0 600 38824 7

First published in Great Britain 1979
by Hamlyn Paperbacks
Copyright © Audrey Ellis 1979

Hamlyn Paperbacks are published by
The Hamlyn Publishing Group Ltd,
Astronaut House,
Feltham,
Middlesex, England.

Made and printed in Great Britain by
Hazell Watson & Viney Ltd, Aylesbury, Bucks

Line drawings by
Tony Streek

Contents

Introduction

In an ideal world you would have all the kitchen equipment you needed, unlimited housekeeping money, and complete success with every recipe. But in real life most of us have to make do with a kitchen which lacks some of the latest gadgets, on a budget which is far from elastic. It goes without saying, too, that dishes do not always turn out exactly as you would hope. That is why a collection of tried and tested hints often comes in handy to help solve your household problems and make life run more smoothly. This is my own collection, made over the last few years, and it contains many a life-saver, like the easy way to separate an egg on a day when you feel all fingers and thumbs, or how to skin a frozen tomato. I am delighted to share my favourite tips with you and I hope this book will become your constant companion in the kitchen.

Audrey Ellis

PART ONE

KITCHEN HINTS

The more you know about the use and maintenance of your precious kitchen equipment the better. If it is used correctly and looked after carefully, you will get the best possible results and have pleasure in using it. There's a great sense of pride in being able to put a plug on your latest new electric gadget safely, and this is just one of the many hints I've included here.

To reduce the necessity for oven cleaning

Ideally the cooker should be wiped down immediately after use with a damp cloth wrung out in warm water with liquid detergent. Cooking in covered dishes whenever possible to keep the oven clean and placing a sheet of foil in the bottom of the oven saves cleaning burnt-on food spills. If very heavily soiled, a proprietary oven cleaner pad or spray may be used.

Cleaning cooker parts with biological detergent

Fill the sink with a strong solution of biological detergent and leave all removable parts of the cooker to soak overnight. Next day, brush lightly and rinse well. Give the same treatment to a heavily-encrusted pan or roasting tin. Or, sprinkle dry biological detergent into a wet pan and leave overnight. Next day, rub with a nylon scouring pad.

Caring for your oven racks

Clean regularly with soap-impregnated steel wool pads. Dip the pad in hot water, fold round each rod, rub up and down briskly to remove all the food particles. Rinse carefully, dry off and apply a little petroleum jelly to the runners to make sure that the rack moves easily. If the runners stick and jolt, delicate items such as a sponge cake or soufflé might sink. Also if you pull a roasting tin of hot fat out on a rack which sticks, the fat might spill and burn you.

Making use of residual oven heat

When main dishes are removed, use leftover heat to dry stale bread for rusks or croûtons. Apple rings, plum and apricot halves, etc., can be dried until leathery then stored. Soak overnight before cooking. Flower petals can be dried until cornflake-crisp to make a pot-pourri.

Keeping a ceramic hob in good condition

Clean every day with the manufacturer's cleanser/conditioner or a cream cleanser to prevent dirt building up. Clean weekly to remove stubborn stains, especially in areas where pan bases rest directly on the heated surface.

Economical use of oven heat and space

Instead of using the oven at regular intervals to bake cakes and frequently placing only one roasting tin or casserole in the oven for a main meal, work out a chart of oven temperatures so that you can see which cakes, pastries and teabreads you can bake at the same time as a main dish. For instance, a meat pie with flaky or puff pastry, or a toad-in-the-hole, needs a high temperature suitable for bread, scones and rock cakes. To prevent sweet dishes from taking up savoury flavours, cover an open meat dish with foil or put your chicken in a roasting bag.

Cooking a vegetable pack in the oven

When using the oven for roasting or baking, cook frozen vegetables in foil packs in the oven instead of in water on top of the cooker. A family-sized portion of peas will take about 30 minutes in a moderately hot oven.

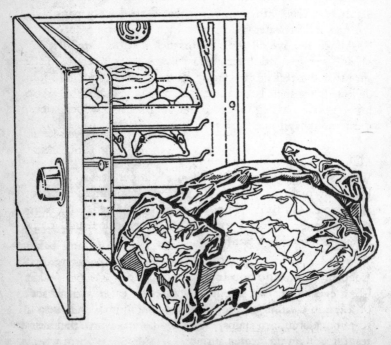

Converting Fahrenheit and Celsius temperatures

To convert °Fahrenheit to °Celsius – deduct 32, multiply the remainder by 5 and divide by 9.

To convert °Celsius to °Fahrenheit – multiply by 9, divide by 5 and add 32.

It is possible to make quick approximate conversions as follows:

From °F to °C – deduct 30 and divide the remainder by 2.

From °C to °F – multiply by 2 and add 30.

To make a magnetic oven or freezer mitt

Buy a small pair of magnets (not horseshoe-shaped) and sew a magnet into each one of a pair of oven mitts or into the centre of a joined pair. The metal should be protected by one thickness of material so that the magnetic attraction is sufficient to hold it firmly against the side of the oven without the risk of burning your fingers against the metal, which is a good conductor of heat.

Quick defrosting for your refrigerator

Combine baking with defrosting. Put clean cake tins, bread tins or baking trays in the freezing compartment while they are still warm after use. Or fill a couple of mixing bowls with really hot water and pop those in instead.

To stop smells in the refrigerator

A small ball of cotton wool dampened with vanilla essence and placed in the refrigerator will stop unpleasant odours for up to a month. After that it will need renewing.

To clean a refrigerator or freezer before storing it

As the door seal on these pieces of equipment is absolutely airtight, this may cause problems. Wash the fridge or freezer out thoroughly with a solution of warm water and baking powder or bicarbonate of soda using 300 ml/½ pint water to 1 teaspoon powder. Dry carefully with a soft cloth, taking special care to dry all the folds of the rubber door seals. Sprinkle these with talcum powder and rub it well into all the crevices. Leave the door open until you are sure the cabinet is completely dry (moisture will cause mildew to form when it is sealed for storage). Place an open container partly filled with bicarbonate of soda in the cabinet before sealing.

Defrosting your freezer

Choose a time when stocks are low, switch off beforehand, then unpack quickly into cardboard cartons, placing all packs which need using up into a separate carton, regardless of the type of food they contain. Place bowls of hot water at strategic points to hasten thawing, remove the frost as it softens (see below), and finish up by wiping the freezer with a cloth dipped in a solution made in the proportion of 1 teaspoon bicarbonate of soda dissolved in 600 ml/1 pint hot water. Wipe with a clean dry cloth. Switch on, close the door and re-plan the placing of stock. Note current stock and replace in the freezer with the basket or box of 'overdue' packs well to the fore.

N.B. To make short work of defrosting the freezer use a clean plastic dustpan and brush. When the freezer has been switched off for long enough to loosen the accumulated ice slightly, chip it off carefully with the edge of the dustpan and sweep it into the pan with the brush. Ideally, keep a new pan and brush specifically for this task, otherwise wash the pan and brush thoroughly in hot water and detergent and let it dry before using.

Drying herbs by microwave

Spread small sprigs or single leaves of herbs on a sheet of soft kitchen paper. Cover with another sheet and microwave for 2 minutes. Strip the leaves from stalks and stems, crumble between your fingers and store in airtight containers. (Woody stemmed herbs such as rosemary may require turning over and processing for a further $\frac{1}{2}$ minute before becoming completely dry.)

Microwave cooking for children

Make an easy and safe beginning for children by allowing them to heat a mug of milk or water in the microwave oven for a hot drink. This takes 2 minutes and the handle of the mug remains cool.

Peeling tomatoes and peaches by microwave

Place the fruit on a sheet of soft kitchen paper and microwave for 30 seconds. Allow to rest for 30 seconds then split the skin at the stalk end and it will peel off easily.

Melting chocolate by microwave

Break up the chocolate and place in a suitable bowl. Cover and microwave for 1 minute. Stir, cover again and repeat as necessary. Stir and heat only until smooth; do not overcook. According to the recipe, chocolate can be melted with butter, margarine, golden syrup, honey, evaporated milk, cream or strong coffee.

To make caramel easily in the microwave

Place 100 g/4 oz granulated sugar and 1 tablespoon water in a suitable container and microwave for about 4 minutes, until the sugar becomes a golden-brown liquid.

To plump dried fruit quickly in the microwave

Place raisins, currants or sultanas in a suitable container and just cover with water. Microwave for 4 minutes, allow to stand for 4 minutes then drain and dry well on soft kitchen paper.

To cook a suet pudding in 10 minutes by microwave

Place 75 g/3 oz sultanas in a suitable basin, cover with water, microwave for 2 minutes. Drain, mix with 50 g/2 oz each self-raising flour, soft breadcrumbs and shredded suet, 25 g/1 oz soft brown sugar, $\frac{1}{2}$ teaspoon ground mixed spice, 1 beaten egg and 3 tablespoons milk. Turn into a suitable greased basin, cover with cling wrap, microwave for 6 minutes. Leave for 2 minutes then turn out.

To toast chopped nuts and breadcrumbs in the microwave

Spread the nuts or breadcrumbs in a thin layer on a plate and microwave for 3 minutes, stirring them every minute.

To poach an egg in the microwave

Place 450 ml/$\frac{3}{4}$ pint water in a suitable basin or shallow container and microwave for 4 minutes. Add $\frac{1}{4}$ teaspoon salt and

1 teaspoon vinegar and carefully slip in one shelled egg. Microwave for 45–60 seconds depending on the size of the egg, until lightly set. Remove with a slotted draining spoon. Cook only one egg at a time, but after removal of the first egg it is possible to add a second egg to the same cooking water.

To scramble an egg in the microwave
Place one shelled egg in a suitable measuring jug or basin and beat lightly. Microwave for 30 seconds and stir well, mashing any lumps. Microwave for a further 30 seconds, stir and mash again and repeat the cooking process if necessary.

To fry an egg in the microwave
Place 15 g/½ oz butter on a suitable plate and microwave for 25 seconds. Slide a shelled egg on to the melting butter and just break the membrane over the yolk of the egg with the tines of a fork. Cover lightly with a sheet of waxed paper or non-stick cooking parchment and microwave for 45–60 seconds, depending on the size of the egg. The egg should still look rather undercooked but will continue to set after removal from the oven if you leave it covered.

Blanching vegetables for freezing by microwave
Prepare 450 g/1 lb vegetables and place in a boiling bag. Add 2 tablespoons water and fold over the top of the bag. Microwave for half the time required by the conventional method. Seal in the usual way and plunge immediately into a bowl of cold water. When cold, dry carefully and freeze.

To speed up total cooking time for barbecued foods
Cook the food items for half the recommended total cooking time in the microwave oven before placing them on the barbecue. This pre-cooking helps the food to cook inside before the outside is over-browned.

Adapting recipes for a crock pot
Remember that roughly only half the usual amount of liquid will be required and reduce quantities of stock, wine, etc., accordingly. To thicken a sauce or gravy, use moistened corn-

flour, stir it in well and allow a further 20 minutes cooking time at the end of the process, otherwise the sauce may taste floury.

Using a tape recorder in the kitchen

If you want to keep a log of certain kitchen jobs without having time to stop working and write down the details, use a tape recorder. When doing experimental cookery, record details of food, measurements and cooking techniques while they are fresh in your mind. When packing the freezer with bulk purchases, record the items and, if required, the prices paid for each of them as you pack the freezer. Later, play back the tapes and write out new recipes neatly, or copy the list of purchases into your freezer record book.

Using a hair drier as a kitchen tool

A hand drier switched to 'cool' can be used for quickly defrosting corners of the freezer or the frozen food storage compartment of a refrigerator. Or, when speed is essential, to dry iced decorations on a cake before proceeding to the next stage of decorating. You can use it to dry washed polythene bags, piping bags and, switched to 'hot', to warm jam jars ready for filling.

Using and maintaining a pressure cooker

Never fill more than two-thirds full, or particles of food will block the valve. Wash immediately after use in warm water containing liquid detergent. If food has stuck to the base, soak in cold water for several hours to loosen. Wash the lid and rubber ring and clean the valve channel under a jet of running water. Wipe the base of the weight to remove any particles which could clog the valve. Dry, and store open. Replace the rubber ring at least every two years, even if the pressure cooker is not frequently used.

Economizing on fuel with a pressure cooker

Certain main dishes, such as boiled fowl or brisket of beef, take a long time to cook by conventional methods. Both are relatively cheap for this reason, and they can be cooked in a short time in a pressure cooker saving cost on the initial purchase and on the use of fuel.

Using and maintaining a mincer
Besides mincing meat, a mincer will chop raw or dried fruit, especially for chutneys, pickles and sauces. It will also mince baked crusts to make browned breadcrumbs for coating food for frying. To prevent it from marking the working surface, place a piece cut from an old rubber mat or bicycle tyre under the clamp. Always wash a new mincer before using. Have a bowl of hot water with liquid detergent ready to wash the small parts and drop them in immediately after use. Rinse and dry very carefully before assembling and storing.

Using the timer on your cooker as a reminder
Pingers are useful for other purposes besides the timing of boiled eggs or a baked soufflé. Set your pinger when getting ready to go to work or when the children should leave for school. When the pinger goes, there's no argument – you, or they, should be going too.

Extra uses for an egg timer
Although it does not take the place of a pinger because it gives no audible alarm, it can be used to time telephone calls and is useful when organizing children's games such as the memory game (when children have three minutes to write down as many items as possible that they have been shown on a tray).

Chopping raw vegetables in a blender
It is usually difficult to process raw vegetables without liquid in the blender so if this is what is required, half-fill the goblet with vegetable pieces and add sufficient cold water to cover the chopping blades. Liquidize until the vegetables are chopped to your liking then turn the mixture into a colander and drain off the water.

Other uses for a potato peeler
This gadget is also useful for peeling other root vegetables,

peeling a cucumber, removing the rind from citrus fruit for marmalade and making chocolate curls, and with practice it can be used for stringing celery and runner beans.

Cutting up marshmallows, glacé cherries, dates, etc.
Use a pair of kitchen scissors for this job. Dip them (and your fingers) into hot water before starting and at intervals.

Opening a can for easy inspection
Always open the end of the can stamped with the manufacturer's code number. If the contents are in any way unsatisfactory, wash and dry the lid and send it to the food company with a note of your comments and the place and date of purchase. This is a great help to the food company in dealing with your complaint.

Storing partly used canned food
Unless the contents are acid, such as some fruits, leave in the can, as the inside is sterile when opened and probably safer than a bowl or jar which has only been washed up. Cover with the lid or with cling wrap and place in the refrigerator, where the contents will keep safely at least for 3 or 4 days.

Opening a can with a wall opener
If the can has a paper wrapper, tear this away before using the can opener, as otherwise the latter may get choked with paper and will not work efficiently.

Cooking in a wok
A favourite cooking utensil of the Chinese is this large pan with sloping sides. It is very quick, economical on fuel, excellent for slimmers and also very good for the health as little fat is needed. It requires a ring to balance it firmly on a modern hob.

How to clean a blender goblet quickly
Fill to one-third full with warm water, add one drop of liquid detergent and switch on for a few seconds to remove any remaining food particles and to facilitate washing.

Making a hay box for emergency cooking
Take a strong cardboard box and line it with hay or other insulating material such as polystyrene tiles or granules. Bring the food to the boil and if possible cook for at least 10 minutes. Place the pan or casserole containing food at boiling point in the centre of the box. Loosely pack any spaces with crumpled newspaper, hay or polystyrene granules and cover the pan with a thick layer. Cover this with the lid of the box and the food will continue to cook for many hours, and will keep hot for up to 12 hours.

Caring for a milk pan
Always rinse out the pan with cold water before using it to heat milk. This helps prevent the milk from sticking to the pan and makes cleaning easier after use. Also, always fill the pan with cold water immediately after use for the same reason.

Caring for an omelette pan
To season it, fill the pan to a depth of 1.5 cm/½ inch with cooking oil. Place over low heat until the oil begins to smoke, remove from the heat and allow the pan to cool. Pour out the oil and keep for frying. Wipe any excess from the inner surface of the pan with soft kitchen paper. Try not to use it for other purposes such as frying, and avoid washing it. Clean it with a few drops of oil on a pad of a soft kitchen paper.

To season ordinary pans cheaply
Pour in cooking salt to form an even layer 1.5 cm/½ inch deep. Place over moderate heat until the salt turns golden brown. Remove from the heat, throw away the salt and wipe the pan clean with soft kitchen paper.

Keeping aluminium pans bright
When using them for steaming or boiling eggs, add a teaspoon of vinegar or a slice of lemon to the water to prevent discoloration. If the pan has become discoloured inside, fill it with water when you are using apples for cooking. Save the peel, add it to the water and boil for 10 minutes. Rinse well with fresh hot water.

Improvising a temporary knob for a saucepan lid

If the original knob was screwed on to the lid, use the existing hole. Insert a screw with a large head through it from the underside and twist a cork down on to the screw. If the knob was stuck to the lid, you will need to drill a hole first.

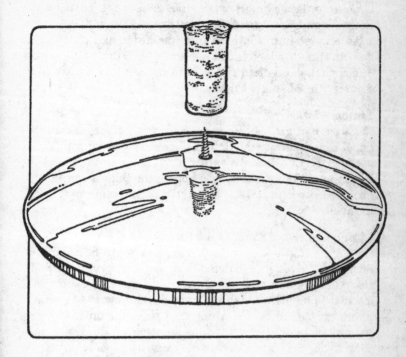

Keeping saucepan lids tidy

Fix a length of plastic-coated curtain wire horizontally on the wall or to the inside of a cupboard door. Slide clean pan lids behind the wire so that the knobs rest on it. Adjust the tension of the wire so that it supports the lids without sagging.

Rejuvenating pans

1 Non-stick pans which become discoloured, especially frying pans, can be restored to their good looks by half-filling

with a solution in the proportion of 1 tablespoon chlorine bleach and 1 tablespoon vinegar to 300 ml/$\frac{1}{2}$ pint water. Bring to the boil, turn off the heat and allow to cool. Empty and wash in the usual way, very thoroughly.

2 To bring back the gleam to darkened aluminium pans, fill with a solution in the proportion of 2 teaspoons cream of tartar to 1 litre/1$\frac{3}{4}$ pints water and simmer for 10 minutes. Empty at once and wash in the usual way.

3 To remove burnt-on food from the inside of a pan with a delicate surface which is not non-stick, soak overnight in salt water, empty and clean gently with dry salt and a nylon pot scourer. Rinse in the usual way.

Lining a Swiss roll tin

Cut a piece of greaseproof paper 5 cm/2 inches larger than the tin all round. Grease the tin and place the paper on top. Press it into place. Cut from the corner of the paper to the corner of the tin in all four corners, overlapping the snipped corners to make the paper fit neatly. Grease the paper before putting in the mixture.

Lining a round or square cake tin

Cut a strip of greaseproof paper long enough to fit round the tin and slightly higher than the sides. Snip at regular intervals along one edge to a depth of 2 cm/$\frac{3}{4}$ inch. Grease the tin and insert the lining strip with the fringed end downwards, easing it into the base of the tin. Using the base of the tin as a guide, cut a circle or square of paper to fit inside the tin neatly, and use it to line the bottom of the tin. Grease the paper again before putting in the cake mixture. To give added protection to large fruit cakes, tie a double layer of brown paper or paper cut from a carrier bag round the outside of the tin, projecting 5 cm/2 inches above it.

Preparing baking sheets when making biscuits

Any biscuit mixture containing syrup, treacle, oatmeal or cheese should be cooked on ungreased baking sheets sprinkled very lightly with flour. All other mixtures should be baked on greased baking sheets. After baking, allow biscuits to cool for a few minutes, until they firm up, before removing to a wire rack.

Time saver when lining cake tins

When cutting out greaseproof paper or non-stick cooking parchment liners for baking tins, mark out on one sheet then cut out through several thicknesses at once and save the spare liners for future use.

Keeping baked potatoes under control in the oven

Arrange scrubbed potatoes for baking in the cups of a bun tin. You can then easily draw out the tin to test whether the potatoes are cooked and they will not stick to the bars of the oven rack. Leftover baked potatoes can be dipped into cold water and re-baked until heated through.

Using 'lifters' to remove food from containers

Before baking such items as fruit cakes, tea breads and pâtés in loaf shaped tins, ensure that they will be easy to remove by inserting a long strip of foil or greaseproof paper folded in three down one narrow side of the tin, along the bottom and up the other narrow side. Leave the ends of the liner sufficiently long to enable the item to be lifted out easily. If necessary, line the tin in the usual way over this and grease well. A lifter can also be placed in a round tin. Use the same principle to remove decorated cakes from storage containers. If the cake has been frozen, remove while still in the frozen state to avoid damage.

Cleaning a fish or chicken brick

These unglazed earthenware utensils are very porous and will absorb the smell of detergent used for washing-up. The best way to clean them is to fill both halves with hot water, add a tablespoon of cooking salt to each and allow to soak for 30 minutes. Stubborn remnants of cooked food can be removed by rubbing briskly with a damp cloth dipped in salt, or with a nylon scouring pad. Rinse well afterwards.

Maintaining earthenware cooking dishes

To prevent cracking during cooking, soak unglazed earthenware dishes in cold water for about 20 minutes, then drain before using. After use, clean as above. Glazed earthenware dishes should be washed in warm water with liquid detergent. If food still adheres to the dish, soak in cool water before washing. Remove stubborn stains by soaking in hot water and soda. Use 1 tablespoon soda to 4 litres/7 pints water.

Cleaning a food grater
Remnants of citrus fruit rinds, etc., seem to cling to the grating surfaces. Flick them out with a clean pastry brush, then wash the grater with a stiff nylon brush in hot water and liquid detergent. This way nothing is wasted and the grater comes clean in a flash.

Cleaning a bulb baster
Avoid allowing fat inside the baster to become cold and harden. While still warm, repeatedly suck up very hot water with detergent into the baster and expel it until really clean, then repeat the process twice with plain hot water.

Cleaning containers with awkward corners
Using sharp scissors, cut part of a soap-filled wire wool pad, hold it with tweezers, dip it in hot water and press it firmly into the corner or crevice, moving it to and fro to dislodge the dirt. Rinse out thoroughly, or if you can't reach the place to be washed because the whole article cannot be immersed in water, fill a plastic water spray with hot water and repeatedly spray out the newly-cleaned crevice.

Making a peppermill turn easily
If it takes brute force to turn your peppermill, it may be that the oil contained in the peppercorns has rusted the thread on the screw. Dismantle the mill and clean the thread with a piece of clean steel wool or a wire brush to remove the rust. Smear a little petroleum jelly over the thread before re-assembling.

Opening a stubborn screw-topped jar
First try opening the jar, gripping it firmly while wearing rubber gloves, or stretching an elastic band round the lid to give you a better grip. If these fail, hold the lid under running

hot water for at least 1 minute so that the metal expands slightly and makes the screw top easier to turn.

Caring for teak salad bowls

Over-frequent washing will remove some of the bowl's colour, make the wood dry and possibly crack. But an occasional quick wash in a mild detergent solution, followed by rinsing and drying, is recommended, because too much oil soaking into the wood eventually turns rancid. After drying, you may polish up the outside of the bowl with a few drops of teak oil on a soft cloth.

Unblocking a kitchen sink pipe

If you have no rubber plunger, use a thick dishcloth or tea towel and place this over the blocked waste hole. Cover the overflow hole with another cloth then exert a strong plunging action with your hand over the waste pipe hole. Or fill the sink half-full and place a plastic seaside bucket or a litre ice-cream carton over the waste hole, trapping air in it. Cover the overflow hole with a cloth then press on the side of the bucket to force air down the pipe. When the blockage has cleared, tip household soda into the pipe to fill it and pour over boiling water. Leave overnight if possible without using the sink.

An easy way to clean the kitchen floor

If you have no squeezy mop, soak a big absorbent floor cloth in a light cleaning solution, wring it out, throw it down and propel it forcefully across the floor with the ball of one foot. Flip the cloth over and work back in the opposite direction. Our mothers probably wouldn't have approved, but this is a real time-and-effort saver.

Repairing plastic kitchen utensils

Repair a large item such as a plastic washing-up bowl which has split by drawing a hot soldering iron or heated skewer along the crack. It will fuse both sides together. Small items such as plastic measuring spoons can often be mended in the same way with a lighted match. The plastic becomes discoloured and the mend will show, but the spoon is safe to use.

Improvising a vegetable piping bag

Greaseproof paper which is suitable for making piping bags for icing will not stand either the weight or heat of, say, hot mashed potato.

1 Make a bag as described on page 97 using double thickness foil, but protect your hands from conducted heat by wearing rubber gloves or by grasping the bag through a clean tea towel. Snip off the end of the bag ready for piping.

2 Cut off one corner diagonally from a heavy gauge polythene bag and insert a piping nozzle. If necessary, slip one bag inside another and use two bags to give extra strength. Fill with the food to be piped and use like a nylon forcing bag.

To fill a piping bag cleanly

Fix the piping nozzle firmly in place, turn back the top half of the bag to make a deep cuff, put the bag into a clean jam jar or jug so that the cuff falls outside it. Fill the bag as far as possible, gently pushing down the contents to avoid air pockets. Pull up the cuff and twist against the contents to force out any remaining air. Fold down the top neatly to hold with one hand while you guide and press out the contents with the other.

Filtering liquids

If you do not possess a sufficiently fine sieve, line the one you have available with a square of cheesecloth or muslin. The finer the mesh of the material, the longer the job will take but the more perfect the result will be.

Improvising iced lolly moulds

Fill dimpled plastic egg boxes with the lolly mixture, insert wooden or plastic lolly sticks and freeze in the usual way.

To improvise small moulds

Cut a circle from a double thickness of foil and smooth it over the base of a suitably-sized tumbler. Peel back and turn down the top edge if necessary. Chill in the refrigerator for a few minutes, then slip out the tumbler. If you have a set of matching tumblers you can make several improvised moulds at the same time.

To improvise a plastic bowl scraper
Remove the raised edge from the firm plastic lid of a margarine tub. Cut the resulting circle in half and use the rounded edge of one half as a scraper.

How to improvise a wash rag from nylon net
Buy this net by the metre or the yard and cut it up into handy-sized squares. It rinses out easily, is tremendously durable and just rough enough to clean without scratching. It costs far less than throw-away cloths.

To improvise a cherry- or grape-stoner
For cherries, use a strong, clean hairpin. Insert the rounded end into the cherry, move it until it locks behind the stone, then jerk sharply to pull out the stone. Do this over a bowl or saucepan as the juice tends to spurt out when the stone is removed. Treat grapes in the same way, using a clean hair-grip to pull out the pips.

Improvising a salt cellar for packed meals
Cut a waxed straw in half, twist one end, fill with salt and twist the other end to close. To use, untwist one end and shake out the salt a little at a time.

Improvising a flour dredger
Punch 5 or 6 holes in the soft metal top of a screw-topped jam jar. You can dredge lightly or thickly according to the number of holes you punch and how big you make them. Or make holes in the top of a plastic jar with a heated skewer for the same purpose.

To improvise a bain-marie
Place the dish of food to be cooked in a deep roasting tin and pour in sufficient boiling water to come half-way up the sides of the dish.

Improvising a tight seal for casseroles
If you have a casserole lid which is not a good fit, cut a long narrow strip of foil and crumple it lightly so that it just fits

round the top of the dish. Shape it to the rim, put the lid in place and press down firmly. If you have no lid at all, cut a piece of foil slightly larger than the casserole, lay it on top and press the edges firmly under the rim.

Improvising an egg poacher
Grease well a number of small foil cake cases and drop an egg into each. Add to a frying pan containing water to come half-way up the depth of the foil cases. Bring to the boil, reduce to simmering point, cover and cook until the eggs are set.

Improvising an insulated container
Line a strong cardboard carton with polystyrene ceiling tiles, trimming them with a sharp knife to fit. Cover the food with a clean cloth, then with newspaper or more tiles. Fold in the flaps with the corners overlapping. If the box is filled with hard-frozen food, it will stay frozen for up to 12 hours. A small insulated box with a lid made in this way can be used to prevent milk which has to be delivered when no one is at home from going 'off' in the heat of the sun.

Improvising a cake board
Draw round the base of a large cake tin or a plate of suitable size on thick cardboard. Cut out and cover with heavy duty foil, shiny side outwards, cutting the foil round a large plate or tin and allowing at least 1.5 cm/½ inch to tuck under. Smooth the cut edges underneath, making sure to eliminate air pockets. You can also cover a damaged cake board in this way.

To improvise a cake tin
Undamaged fruit cans, which have been opened with a can opener which leaves a smooth edge, can be used as cake tins, producing cakes which look unusual and attractive when cut in round slices.

Improvising a filter for a coffee pot
Use a strong white 'man-size' paper tissue to line the container for the coffee grounds. Not only is the coffee filtered but the used grounds are easy to lift out of the pot afterwards.

Improvising dividers for freezing

Save the waxed paper liners from cereal cartons and cut them up neatly into convenient sizes to use as dividers. Pierced polythene bags which cannot be re-used for their original purpose can also be cut up and used in this way. If you still have trouble separating food items in the frozen state, use two dividers instead of one.

Improvising freezer containers

Many take-away food containers are made of foil and if carefully washed and pressed back into shape while still warm can be used for freezing home-prepared meals. Bakeries also sell flans in re-usable foil dishes. Save all of these and use sheet foil to seal them with.

Improvising trays for open-freezing

Baking tins are often used but few of us have sufficient for the purpose. Some confectioners have sweets supplied in trays which are not strong enough for baking but are quite suitable for open freezing. Even household trays can be used providing they are clean and dry. To make any tray or flat surface hygienic, cover it with clean foil or polythene.

To improvise labels for freezer packs

Write a description of the food on a sheet of plain paper and slip it inside a polythene bag with the food so that it is easy to read through the bag. If the food to be packed is damp, such as a joint or decorated cake, open freeze before packing.

Improvising a blanching basket

Most vegetables require to be blanched before freezing and if you do not have a special blanching basket use a wire frying basket for large items such as Brussels spouts or a clean nylon net shopping bag for small items such as peas. If you have neither, blanch the vegetables loose in the blanching water and retrieve with a slotted draining spoon or small metal sieve.

Planning a kitchen for maximum convenience

Plan the position of large pieces of equipment to save walking to and fro, stretching up, and opening and closing doors unnecessarily. Plot the cook's progress from the store cupboard and the refrigerator to the worktop, and from the worktop to the sink and the cooker, having the serving area nearest to the hatch or dining-room. Store the most used food items (tea, coffee, flour, sugar) at hand-height, and the most used crockery (teacups, saucers, mugs) on the most accessible cupboard shelves. Relegate foods and utensils not so frequently needed to top shelves or low storage space which involves stooping. The height of a working surface should be calculated to avoid fatigue. About 82.5 cm/33 inches is average, but test the height by standing in front of your worktop. You should be able to rest the palms of your hands on it without bending your elbows. Working on a surface that is too high constantly demands extra exertion and is tiring; working on one that is too low is likely to give you backache.

Wiring a plug
Undo the screw holding together the two parts of the plug. Separate the three wires and pass under the small holding bar into the plug. Expose just sufficient bare wire to connect to the appropriate screws.

The brown wire is live	L
The blue wire is neutral	N
The green/yellow wire is earth	E

Connect the wires to the appropriately marked terminals: brown to the fused right-hand side; blue to the unfused left-hand side; green/yellow to the top screw. Make sure that they are firmly attached. Screw down the holding bar to keep the wire firmly in place, then replace the plug cover and screw it down firmly.

Using an old toothbrush or nail brush as a kitchen utensil
Wash well, sterilize if possible in a Milton solution, and use for cleaning awkwardly-shaped vegetables. (Remember, it's better not to peel them if you can avoid it since so much nutritional value hides just under the skin.) These brushes are also marvellous to clean round the bases of kitchen taps, or as silver polishers for decorated embossed cutlery.

To keep sharp knives safe in a drawer

Stick the tips into clean wine corks, or block the end of an inner cardboard tube from a roll of foil with a large cork and slip long knives into it. Use a similar tube from a toilet roll for small vegetable knives.

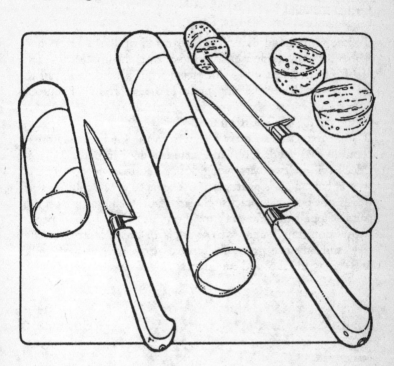

Safety tips in the kitchen

Always wipe up food spills, especially greasy ones, from the kitchen floor at once. A skid followed by a fall can cause a nasty accident, involving cuts from broken china and glass or sharp cutlery, or burns from hot food.

Beating food safely and quietly

Place a folded damp tea towel under the bowl to prevent it from slipping while you use the beater, and also to reduce the noise.

To save trouble when mincing food

To mince and pack in one operation, place a polythene bag over the end of the mincer and secure it in place with an elastic band. Mince the food straight into the bag, and when full enough it can easily be removed and the contents weighed without further handling.

To keep mirror surfaces from steaming up in the kitchen

Rub a little glycerine well into the mirror, then polish up with a soft cloth. Even a blast of steam from a kettle will fail to mist it over. (The same hint applies in the bathroom, of course.)

Safety tip for transporting food

If you often have to carry a tray from the kitchen to another room (a two-handed job) and there is a door in between, consider having a two-way swing door fitted to save accidents. It should have a glass porthole at eye level to avoid collisions. If this is not possible, practise the art of balancing a tray on the palm of one hand, fingers spread out, as a waiter does! Begin with a non-fragile item such as a loaf of bread centred on the tray, and advance gradually towards carrying a teapot, milk jug, etc., with grace and confidence.

PART TWO

HOUSEKEEPING HINTS

Getting the best value for your money is an important aspect of the good housekeeper's art. So you need to know how to shop well and plan the most delicious menus without being extravagant over food. In this section there are many helpful tips including some on dry goods and freezer storage, and coping with everyone's unfavourite task, the washing-up.

Be a realistic shopper

Stick to your shopping list, restricting extra purchases to 'loss leaders' which are offered as a bargain to lure you into the store in the first place. But bargains not to be passed up are those items reduced in price because the safety time limit is about to expire. However, take the time limit seriously and use up the bargain item quickly.

Get the goods home safely

Check regularly that your shopping bag/basket/trolley is in good condition. Don't overload it and suffer a sudden collapse which spills breakables all over the pavement. Remember it is less strain to carry two bags of shopping, evenly balanced, than one large bag 'listing to starboard'. Make sure your purse and handbag are safe repositories for your money, too. Money can just fall out by mistake or may be extracted by a light-fingered pickpocket who preys on careless shoppers.

Check what food costs

To make a survey of where your money goes occasionally take a pencil with you and actually fill in the prices on your shopping list as you tick off the items bought. This takes a little extra time and trouble but may show where you are over-spending. For example, you might be paying out over £1.00 a week for fancy biscuits when you could make the same weight for approximately one-third of the price at home. The money saved might be better spent on more fruit or vegetables.

Weighing up relative values in food

Size is not an instant indication of value for money. Small cans of condensed soup may hold twice as much as regular cans of ordinary soup. A big pack of biscuits may weigh light and contain less in 'biscuit value' than a small pack of heavier biscuits.

Economy hints on buying vegetables

Do not judge entirely by the price charged by weight. If vegetables are dirty or not carefully trimmed, you may be paying almost half your money for rubbish which you have to discard after the effort of carrying it home. For example, untrimmed leeks are frequently one-third waste and so is the heavy core with its coarse leaves at the base of an inadequately trimmed cabbage. If necessary, weigh the trimmings and convince yourself how much you have paid for sheer waste. Since cabbage is the green vegetable most frequently bought all round the year, become a cabbage connoisseur. If the cabbage looks fresh but is yellower in colour than it should be, the stale outer leaves may have been stripped off. The 'heart' may be quite tasty but it will need to be used with all speed.

Shopping economically for perishables

Just before shops close for early closing day, or for the weekend, fresh produce is often sold off cheaply. Prepare it as soon as you can, and blanch and freeze any surplus, being sure to cut out and discard damaged parts such as the bruised portions of fruit.

Choosing fruit

Whenever possible, choose fruit individually, but if this is not possible look for brightly-coloured, smooth, unshrivelled fruit without bruises or blemishes. Good citrus fruit is usually heavy for its size and the ripeness of a pear can be judged by its skin colour and whether the stalk is easily pulled away. With experience it is possible to judge how long unripe fruit should be kept in a warm place to bring it to perfection. It is wiser to buy slightly under-ripe fruit rather than risk it spoiling before you need it.

Choosing meat

Veal, lamb and pork do not require long hanging in order to become tender and develop a good flavour. They are at their best when the flesh is pink in colour and the fat is white or pale cream. There should not be too much fat and the rind of pork should be smooth and not too thick. Beef requires longer hanging, usually about 10 days, by which time the flesh may be dark red and the fat yellowish. A good butcher will tell you whether any meat has been properly hung. When meat is pre-packed, try to avoid packages containing fatty cuts hidden beneath an attractive piece on top.

Storage: minced meat and offal should not be kept longer than one day even in the refrigerator. Large joints will keep for three to five days.

Items to buy ahead

If possible, buy soap and candles in bulk and store them until required. They will harden with keeping and last longer when brought into use. You will get more use from each bar of soap and each candle will burn steadily for a longer period of time than a candle which has not been stored.

To save running out of essential foods

Have a wipe-away memo board prominently placed on your kitchen wall. Get into the habit of writing on it any food which is low in stock before it quite runs out and get all the rest of the family to do this too. It's the person who actually digs deep into the cereal packet who knows it is nearly empty! Consult the memo board each time you make up your shopping list.

To remove traces of pesticides, etc., from fruit and vegetables

Add 2 tablespoons of vinegar to a bowl of cold water and use to soak fruit or vegetables for 15 minutes. Clean lightly with a brush then rinse and dry. Polish up hard fruit with a clean cloth before placing it in the fruit bowl.

Making food preparation easier

Place a large jug filled with hot water and liquid detergent close by when you cook. Plunge large knives, forks, spoons, spatulas, etc., straight into the jug after use. They will only require a quick rinse to be ready for action again immediately.

Weighing foods without mess

When the ingredients of a recipe are to be gradually added to a saucepan or bowl, place the pan or bowl on the scales first and note the weight. Then add the various items while the pan is sitting on the scales. Keep fats such as butter in their wrappings when you weigh them to avoid making the scale pan greasy. The weight of the wrappings can be disregarded. To weigh sticky foods, line the scale pan with a square of foil, grease-proof paper or freezer tissue which can be lifted out with the food, leaving the pan clean. Sprinkle a light dusting of flour on the scale pan before weighing sticky foods like figs, glacé cherries, and so on.

To save trouble when preparing vegetables
Stand a colander in a bowl of cold water. Dip the vegetables in the water and peel or scrape them into the colander. Drop the prepared vegetables into a separate pan of water. When preparation is complete, you can lift out all the peelings together in the colander and need only tip out dirty water from the bowl down the sink.

How to answer the bell without leaving floury fingerprints
Whenever you are making pastry, or doing other jobs which make your fingers floury, keep two polythene bags open and ready to slip over your hands if the doorbell goes or the telephone rings. It is sometimes useful to don the polythene bags to protect long fingernails, a painful cut or a freshly-applied manicure, before you begin rubbing fat into flour.

How to keep recipe books clean in the kitchen
Prevent the cover of your favourite book from becoming marked by sticky fingers by covering the outside smoothly with cling wrap. You will still be able to see the cover through the transparent wrap which gives excellent protection.

Using a vacuum flask as a fuel saver
Foods which cook by simmering, especially soups, can be partly cooked, then transferred to a vacuum flask which has been rinsed out with very hot water, to finish cooking. Three hours in the flask is worth another 15 minutes cooking time and the soup stays hot enough to serve immediately for hours longer if a meal is delayed.

To remove food from cans easily
Turn the can over and open the end which has been pointing downwards. Not only is this more hygienic because the surface

will not be dusty, but the food will slip out of the can more easily. For this reason, store cans numbered end downward.

Heating baby's food easily
Keep an egg poacher especially for baby, washing it with extra care after use. Spoon sweet and savoury foods into separate cups and reheat them all in the same pan. In a four-cup poacher you could heat a meat course, two separate vegetables and a pudding at the same time.

Organizing the service of a hot meal
If it is beyond the capacity of your cooker to have several hot dishes ready at the same time, try to prepare sauces or gravy in advance and keep them hot in vacuum flasks. This is also helpful if you do not have sufficient pots and pans. If you have no vacuum flasks, transfer cooked sauces, such as custard or gravy, to boiling bags and keep them hot by popping them into a pan cooking green vegetables, potatoes or pasta.

Planning a well-balanced menu
Choose the main dish first and plan the vegetables to accompany it as a contrast to the first course, and to provide balance with the sweet course. For example, do not serve a salad with the main dish if the first course is a fish cocktail garnished with lettuce, and do not cook Brussels sprouts tossed with almonds if there are nuts in the dessert.

Catering for a slimmer in the family
Instead of thickening dishes at the beginning of cooking (coating diced meat in flour, for instance) reserve all thickening for the end of cooking time. Use moistened cornflour or *beurre manié* and remove the slimmer's portion first. Prepare two green vegetables, and give the slimmer both of these, reserving potatoes or other starchy extras for non-slimmers. If possible, provide an individual side salad for the slimmer. It also helps to always serve out food on small plates, using dessert plates for main courses and bread plates for desserts. The same applies to cold drinks containing calories, such as orange juice and milk. A little looks a lot in a small glass. Buy wafer-

thin crispbreads, and small size loaves of bread. Often slimmers allowed one crispbread or slice of bread will accept a portion which weighs less and therefore contains fewer calories. (See also page 126.)

Catering for an invalid

Doctors' instructions can be confusing. Here are some useful basic rules.

1 *Fat-free diet*: cut out cream, butter, cheese, margarine, fat from meat, oily fish and even egg yolks. Use skimmed milk rather than whole milk.

2 *Low-salt diet*: omit salt from cooked foods, and use unsalted margarine and butter at the table. For cakes, use sodium-free baking powder with plain flour. Most chemists carry a range of salt substitute and packaged salt-free foods. Avoid salty foods such as bacon and smoked fish.

3 *Gastric diet*: omit spices from cooking. Do not offer fruit with pips, vegetables with tough fibres or whole-grain cereals. Avoid smoked foods, fried foods and either very hot or very cold foods. Only offer weak tea and coffee, and no alcohol.

Catering for outdoor meals and picnics

Disposable paper plates and cups save trouble, but for once-only use the cost is considerable. They cost less if you buy small sizes of both plates and cups in large packs, which works out far cheaper per item. It also pays to buy the smaller sized paper napkins in large packs. Save used cream and yogurt pots to serve as throwaway containers for salads and other messy foods (remember not to throw them away until you get home). It is often easier to serve an outdoor meal without argument or spills if each person's meal is wrapped and placed in a labelled plastic bag together with eating implements.

Working out oven temperatures

To keep conversions from Fahrenheit to Celsius easy and yet as accurate as possible, it is necessary to omit the equivalent for 130°C, 170°C and 210°C. The table opposite gives the most satisfactory results.

Description	Degrees Celsius	Degrees Fahrenheit	Gas Mark
Very cool	110	225	$\frac{1}{4}$
	120	250	$\frac{1}{2}$
Cool	140	275	1
	150	300	2
Moderate	160	325	3
	180	350	4
Moderately hot	190	375	5
	200	400	6
Hot	220	425	7
	230	450	8
Very hot	240	475	9

American measures explained

The American pint measures 16 fl oz.
The American cup holds 8 fl oz.
The American tablespoon holds 14.2 ml and is slightly smaller than the Imperial tablespoon which holds 17.3 ml and the large metric spoon which holds 15 ml.

Solid measures using spoons and cups

Taking 25 g/1 oz as a useful basic requirement in cooking, here is the approximate equivalent using 15 ml spoons/tablespoons and American cups.

	15 ml spoons/ tablespoons	American cups
Butter	1½	⅛ cup (2 American table-spoons)
Breadcrumbs (dried)	6	¼ cup
Breadcrumbs (fresh)	7	½ cup
Cornflour	2	¼ cup cornstarch
Flour	3	¼ cup sifted
Rice	2	⅛ cup
Sugar (castor)	2	⅛ cup granulated
Sugar (demerara)	2	⅛ cup, brown, firmly packed
Sugar (icing)	4	¼ cup sifted confectioner's

3 teaspoons equal 1 tablespoon

Wine bottle sizes and pub measures

Measure (spirits) – 22 ml/$\frac{4}{5}$ fl oz
Measure (liqueurs) – 22 ml/$\frac{4}{5}$ fl oz
Miniature bottles – 2–3 tablespoons
Standard half bottle – 350–375 ml/about 13 fl oz
Standard bottle – 700–750 ml/about 1$\frac{1}{3}$ pints
Litre bottle – 1$\frac{3}{4}$ pints
2-litre bottle – 3$\frac{1}{2}$ pints
Half gallon flagon – about 2.3 litres/4 pints
Champagne bottle – 800 ml/1 pint and 8 fl oz
Magnum – 2 standard bottles

Liquid measures using spoons

Spoon measures give an approximate measure only but they
are useful for small quantities.
3 teaspoons = 1 tablespoon
2 tablespoons = about 35 ml/1 fl oz
1 teaspoon = about 5 ml
1 tablespoon = about 17.3 ml
8 tablespoons = about 150 ml/$\frac{1}{4}$ pint

Saving time on preparing stews

The many ingredients requiring to be prepared often make the
work of getting together a stew more trouble than a roast
joint. When preparing a variety of vegetables, cut up extra and
put a selection into a freezer pack to produce next time you
want to make a stew quickly. (Typical selection: carrot, leek,
onion, swede, turnip.) Pop in a bouquet garni and you have
all the hard work except chopping up the meat already done.

Making use of melted frost from your freezer or refrigerator

The melted frost becomes distilled water which you can use for
your steam iron, electric hair rollers or for topping up a car
battery. The water must be absolutely clean.

Saving kitchen discards for the garden

1 Keep empty cardboard egg boxes and use these filled with
suitable compost when it is time to plant seedlings. The cardboard containers keep the seedlings moist and warm.

2 Save cracked nut shells and use these instead of broken crocks to give drainage in the bottom of flower pots.

3 Save empty jam jars and place them over small outdoor plants to protect them from inclement weather.

4 Save wooden lolly sticks to use as plant markers.

To improvise a non-spill drink container for children

If your child is too young to be trusted with a drink in a glass which might be spilled, put the drink into a clean, strong, glass jar with an undamaged screw top. Puncture the top from the outside inwards and insert a drinking straw, preferably the type which bends, making sure that it reaches almost to the bottom of the jar. If you feel you cannot trust your child with a glass container of any kind, use a plastic tumbler with a seal and puncture a hole in the top with a hot skewer.

Re-using empty washing-up liquid containers

After removing all traces of detergent, fill these with fresh water and use to water pot plants or hanging baskets of plants. Filled with sand and then sealed again the containers also make skittles for children's games. Or remove the cap and cut off the top half of the container. Use this as a funnel and the bottom half as a holder for light items such as pencils and a supply of tie-write tags for the freezer.

To check whether polythene bags are re-usable

Fill the bag with water, and grip the top. Water will spurt out through even the smallest hole. If the bags are in good condition, reverse and dry them over clean milk bottles, then peg a collection of the same size together at one corner and pull one out when required.

Cleaning polythene bags

Squeeze a drop of washing-up liquid into the bag, half-fill with hot water and rub between your hands. Rinse out with fresh hot water, turn inside out and stand over a clean milk bottle to dry. To remove persistent odours, dissolve $\frac{1}{2}$ teaspoon of dry mustard in the hot rinsing water, then rinse again and dry as above.

Finding a use for broken china

Sometimes a pretty cup or mug cannot be mended sufficiently to hold water, or the handle is missing and cannot be refixed firmly. The mended article can be used as a cover for a more practical flower container. If crockery is broken beyond repair, save the pieces to use as drainage crocks in plant pots.

To improvise a kitchen scoop

You will need an empty plastic fabric conditioner bottle with a handle. Keep the screw-top in place and lay the bottle on its side with the handle uppermost. Using a serrated knife, saw down the centre of the bottle half-way towards the base, then trim off the sides and end to make a scoop shape.

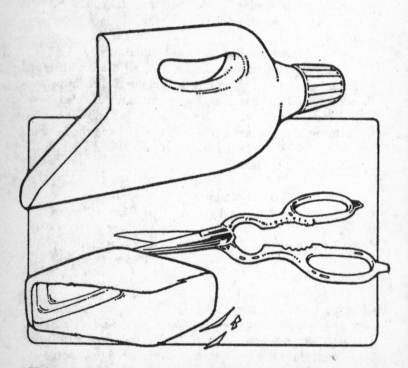

Using up empty ice-cream containers

Round tubs can be carefully cleaned and used again for home freezing, but do not necessarily give a perfect seal when re-used. The large rectangular cartons can also be re-used in the same way, or can be cut up with scissors to make strong dividers which will stand washing and re-using many times.

Re-using screw-topped jars
Fix the lids underneath the base of a wall cupboard or shelf, using one screw through the centre of each. Re-label the jars and store by screwing up into the tops. These are particularly useful for spices and dried herbs, or for storing sewing aids such as needles, pins and buttons.

To sterilize containers for home-made baby foods
Wash the chosen containers and then rinse with the same sterilizing solution used for baby's bottles.

Uses for citrus fruit peels in the house
Place strips of peel in a heat-proof container, fill up with boiling water, cool, seal and keep for up to one week in the refrigerator. Use the scented water as a hair rinse, or to add fragrance to a bath. Place strips of peel to dry (for fire lighters) in the airing cupboard and they impart a delicate scent to the household linen while they are drying. Alternatively, save the peel in a plastic bag, pierced in a number of places, and dry off in the airing cupboard, or on a shovel in the grate when the fire is burning. Grapefruit, lemon, lime and orange rinds all have slightly different and exotic fragrances. For other uses for citrus fruit peel see page 102. Try placing a dried strip of orange or lemon peel in the tea caddy to scent the tea – much cheaper than buying exotic blends. The pips from squeezed lemons can be added to salted water and used to clean inside glass vases or awkwardly-shaped bottles.

To use laddered tights in the kitchen
Laddered tights make good liners for pedal bins (for dry waste only, of course). Cut off the legs a few inches below the gusset, tie the legs together and stretch the waistband over the top edge of the bin.

Economizing on wire twist ties for bags
Shop around and work out whether you get more tying

capacity from those long green plant ties sold in chain stores and garden centres rather than those purely for freezing. Cut the long ones in half and use them for all small packs which only require a short length to seal the bag. And remember to save the plastic tabs used for sealing bread bags as these can be used for the same purposes as twist ties.

To save wasting plastic cling wrap

Small pieces are frequently needed to cover such items as jam jars and tumblers for storage in the refrigerator. Cut a standard-sized roll in half, using a sharp knife with a serrated cutting edge, to provide two small rolls approximately 15 cm/6 inches wide. Replace together in the carton so that you can draw out and pull off short lengths cleanly.

Re-using foil

To clean a large piece of foil for re-use, soak in hot water with detergent, clean gently with a soft brush under the surface of the water, rinse under running hot water then smooth out with a soft cloth on a flat surface while still warm. Once the foil is cold, it tends to tear when you attempt to smooth out creases.

Saving ways with broken biscuits

Broken sweet or semi-sweet biscuits often become stale in the tin and are just thrown away. Have a container marked 'broken biscuits' in the freezer, and add to the contents until you have enough to make an ice-cream freezer cake, or an uncooked refrigerator cake layered with buttercream. Crush the biscuits and mix well together before using in this way. (Broken plain biscuits can be rolled down to make a crumb coating for frying or a topping for oven-baked dishes.)

To use a cake which has become stale and dry

Wrap the cake in foil and warm it in the oven. Unwrap and pour over it a syrup made in the proportion of 8 tablespoons sugar and 1 tablespoon lemon juice to 7 tablespoons water. (If liked, stir in 2 tablespoons sherry). Allow to soak for at least 1 hour before serving.

To freshen crisp foods which have softened

Spread out on a baking sheet and reheat as follows:

1 Semi-sweet biscuits and plain crackers – place in a cool oven (150°C, 300°F, Gas Mark 2) for about 5 minutes. When cool the biscuits or crackers will be crisp.

2 Potato crisps – place in a moderately hot oven (190°C, 375°F, Gas Mark 5) for about 3 minutes. Cool on the baking sheet.

To get the last spoonful out of a sauce bottle

Screw on the top well and stand the bottle upside down, supported if necessary in a jar to prevent it from toppling over. When all the sauce has drained down to the lid end, reverse, unscrew quickly and pour out before the sauce has time to drain back towards the base of the bottle.

To extract the maximum from food in tubes

Tomato purée, processed cheese, condensed milk and pâté are among the foods available in tubes. It is usually recommended to keep the tubes, once opened, in the refrigerator. To make the last few squeezes easier, hold the tube under running hot water for about 10 seconds. If it remains stubborn repeat the process for a further 10 seconds.

To use up broken meringues

These sweet confections are so delicate they break very easily when handled. Crush up any broken meringues, stir into whipped cream flavoured with vanilla and freeze: the resulting ice-cream has a delicious texture. Use the same method with broken macaroons, sweet wafer biscuits and chopped toasted nuts.

To use up syrup from cans of fruit

Make custard to go with the fruit using syrup instead of part of the milk, or use it instead of part of the water to make a jelly. Or add it to a savoury sauce to make a sweet-and-sour version.

Using left-over cooked vegetables as meal starters

Cooked vegetables from the following list make interesting

meal starters if chilled in French dressing and served with lemon and parsley as a garnish: aubergines, beans – including broad, French and runner, cauliflower, celeriac, celery, courgettes, fennel, leeks and also sautéed or raw mushrooms.

Pre-soaking pans before washing

As soon as possible after use, soak pans or dishes used for milk, eggs, cornflour or flour mixtures in *cold* water for at least 20 minutes, as hot water tends to set starchy foods and makes them difficult to remove. Wash in warm soapy water and rinse as usual before putting away.

Removing marks from stainless steel cutlery

If marks are not removed by washing-up, soak the cutlery in a solution of Milton in the proportion of 1 teaspoon to 300 ml/ $\frac{1}{2}$ pint water. To avoid marks on stainless steel cutlery, it is advisable to keep a jug of hot water with a little detergent in the sink during a meal and immediately plunge the used cutlery into it when you clear the table. This prevents stains from 'setting' and makes washing-up much easier.

Washing cutlery with wooden or bone handles

After use, stand in a jug of hot water with liquid detergent but do not immerse the handles or they will eventually become loosened and the surface damaged. Wooden handles may be partly restored by rubbing with teak oil. They are not suitable for the dishwasher, unless guaranteed by the maker.

Washing bone china and porcelain

Take care to use a mild solution of warm water and detergent liquid, as strong detergent may spoil the colour and glaze and remove any gilding. Rinse in clean warm water, then dry and polish with a soft tea towel. Though most china can be placed in a dishwasher, it is advisable to wash valuable china by hand, particularly if decorated with gold leaf or other precious metal. Never place the plates in the oven or under a grill.

Removing tannin stains

Rub stains inside teacups vigorously with salt on a damp cloth and then rinse thoroughly. Soak nylon tea strainers in a strong solution of hot water and washing up liquid for 30 minutes, then clean gently with a nylon brush. Rinse well.

To clean a china or earthenware teapot
Add 2 teaspoons household soda to the empty teapot and fill with boiling water. Allow to stand until just warm then clean with a brush and rinse well. If the spout is clogged by large tea leaves, do not rinse out the pot itself, but hold the spout under fast-running water until the pot is full, then tip out the water.

To remove garlic odour from utensils
Garlic can leave a lingering smell on boards and knives. Rub with salt after use then rinse in cold water before washing in the usual way.

To remove bubble-gum or chewing-gum from fabrics
Put the item in the freezer for at least 3 hours, and the gum can then be cleanly peeled off without leaving a stain.

Improvising a pan scrubber from net food bags
Collect nylon net bags from your purchases of nuts or beans, crumple up about six of them and place inside the stiffest one you have. Tie the end tightly to make a firm pad. Use to clean pans with plenty of scouring cream.

To prevent soap-filled cleaning pads from going rusty
Put the pad in a small polythene container, cover with hot water and seal. When using the pad, always rinse it out well and return it to the sealed container after use. It will stay rustfree until all the soapy liquid in the container is gone. Add a little more water to keep the same pad going for at least a week.

Saving trouble when bleaching
If your kitchen sink would benefit from bleaching, soak items such as stained tea towels, kitchen sponges and dish cloths in soap powder and bleach in the sink overnight, rather than in a bowl. This method performs two jobs at once.

To extend the life of rubber gloves

When new, turn them inside out and stick pieces of adhesive plaster across the fingertips. If you have long nails, small pieces of cotton wool inserted into the fingertips will lessen the risk of puncturing the material.

To repair small tears in rubber gloves

Check where the puncture is by filling the glove with water. Hold the top closed and water will squirt out through the hole. Mark the hole, then dry the glove completely. Stick a small waterproof plaster over the tear on the *outside* of the glove.

Caring for fine wine glasses

Wash in hand-hot water with a little liquid detergent. Rinse in very hot water and drain thoroughly. While still hot, dry using two smooth clean tea towels and both hands, one polishing inside the bowl and the other outside. Hold each glass up to the light to check that no smears are left.

Separating glasses which stick together

Place the bottom glass in hot water and pour cold water into the top glass. After a few moments the glasses should easily come apart. Do not use either boiling or iced water or you risk cracking your glasses.

To wrap glasses safely for storage

Wash and dry the glasses carefully. Wrap them individually in tissue paper or newspaper and lie side by side in alternate rows, rims to bases. Separate the rows with several sheets of crumpled paper. Strong cardboard dividers may also be used – those from wine cases are ideal for this purpose. After prolonged storage, wash again to remove any dust.

Storing bone china and porcelain

Protect plates and saucers stored in piles by interleaving with soft kitchen paper. Avoid storing fine cups by hanging on hooks as the weight may be too much for the delicate handles. Allow plenty of space as breakages may occur in a cramped cupboard, and do not pile up stacks of plates so that the weight on the plate at the bottom of the pile becomes excessive.

Storing potatoes successfully

To prevent potatoes from turning green during storage, pack them in a strong paper bag or sack or a cardboard carton and store in the dark. Do not leave for long in a plastic bag as this retains moisture and encourages the potatoes to rot.

Storing onions safely

Sacrifice an old, clean, pair of tights or stockings. Slip an onion into one toe, tie a knot above it and insert another onion. Repeat the process until each leg is almost full, leaving enough top above the last knot in which to make a hole so that the onion string can hang from a hook. Single onions can be snipped off with scissors as required and if one onion goes rotten it does not affect the others.

Improvising storage shelves for small items

A cutlery box placed on its side in a cupboard gives narrow shelves suitable for storing spice jars, etc.

Storing food in cupboards

Where sufficient cupboards are available, tins and jars are best kept out of sight and away from dust. When the cupboards are very deep, a 'Lazy Susan', which you can turn to bring items at the back to the front, is invaluable. Providing jars are not placed right at the front of cupboard shelves, small narrow shelves may be fitted to the insides of the cupboard doors for extra storage. If sliding doors make this impractical, shallow inner shelves may sometimes be fitted between deep shelves which are far apart. When there is no room in cupboards, such items as rice, flour and pulses should if possible be transferred from bags or cardboard containers to clean jars with well fitting lids. Old coffee or fruit juice jars are useful for this purpose. The lids can easily be painted or covered with adhesive plastic material to make a matching set. Ideally canned goods should be turned top to bottom occasionally during long storage. Always label contents of jars with adhesive labels clearly written, as some items can get confused, particularly flour, cornflour and arrowroot.

To keep a ball of kitchen string tidy

Select a strong plastic bag just the right size to hold the ball of string. Put it in with the end hanging out at the top and fix a twist tie firmly round the mouth of the bag so that you can pull the string out without removing the ball from the bag. It prevents the string from becoming tangled with other items in a drawer. Alternatively, wash a suitably-sized tin (a syrup tin is ideal) and punch a hole in the top large enough to allow the string to pass through easily. Put the ball of string in the tin, threading the end through the hole in the lid, then press the lid on firmly.

Avoiding waste for store-cupboard items

It proves expensive in the long run if you have to throw away items you have hoarded until they are past their best. At least once every month, check through unused items, particularly ones where the seal is broken, and bring survivors from several past inspections well to the fore. Try and use up these items before you buy more of the same, because it is always a temptation to use fresh foods and neglect older packs already in stock. Make a quick list of items that are in danger of spoiling, such as dried fruits that start to crystallize, and tape it to the inside of the cupboard door as a reminder to use them soon.

To make a cheap lining for drawers and shelves
Use ready-pasted vinyl wallpaper. One roll goes much further than a smaller roll of adhesive backed plastic, costs much less, and lasts almost as long. Single rolls in an end-of-line pattern are often sold off at a give-away price.

Improvising kitchen storage
Keep an eye open at the greengrocer's for items he does not want to keep which you might find useful. He will probably be glad to give you net bags from carrots for bulk-bagging items for the freezer, or tissues from wrapped lemons and other fruit which are useful for greasing pans, mopping up spills, etc.

To avoid freezer smells when open-freezing vegetables
Spread the items on a baking sheet and enclose the whole thing in a large polythene bag. Place the tray directly on a freezing shelf or on the base of the fast freezing compartment to ensure the fastest possible freezing.

Freezing liquids in small quantities
Stock, gravy or sauces are sometimes required in small quantities, but not as small as ice cubes. Freeze them in bun tins which provide cubes of about 4 tablespoons, a very handy amount. The blocks can easily be released by knocking the bun tin sharply on the table top. Pack several together in a small polythene bag.

Freezing purées in bags
To make neat cube shapes easy to stack, use small gussetted bags. Press open at the base with your clenched fist and turn back the top all round to make a deep cuff. Spoon in the purée until the bag is half full. Open freeze until firm, then pull up the cuff, draw together and seal tightly with a twist tie.

Freezing custard successfully
Canned custard can be frozen in trifles and other made-up dishes without separating because it is more fully homogenized than home-made custard. It also has the advantage of not forming a skin when exposed to the air when required as a pouring sauce.

Freezing rosettes of whipped cream
If you have a small quantity of whipped cream left in a piping bag, pipe it out on to a sheet of foil or non-stick paper on a baking sheet. Open-freeze then lift off the rossttes with a knife and place them in polythene containers, or cut the lining into squares and pack the rosettes complete with backing sheets. When required for use, remove the frozen rosettes from their backing, put in place and allow about 15 minutes to defrost.

To freeze fruit for wine making
Freeze fruit in polythene bags when it is available for later use in wine making. Since freezing makes some fruit go mushy, the crushing process is easier after defrosting.

Keeping milk in the freezer
Only freeze homogenized milk which has the cream evenly dispersed throughout. Do not freeze in bottles but transfer to polythene containers or freeze in the form of cubes. When frozen, remove from ice cube trays and store in polythene bags. One average cube is sufficient for a cup of tea.

Quick cooling for blanched vegetables
If sufficient ice cubes are not available to help chill blanched vegetables quickly, pre-freeze Freezella or similar bags and put one in the cold water used to cool the vegetables.

To 'chop' frozen herbs quickly
If necessary, transfer the herbs from the pack to a small poly-thene bag. Rub the bag briskly between your hands to crumble the herbs. If they are frozen into a solid block, rub it against the side of a coarse grater. You can then remove as much as you need and replace the frozen block in the freezer.

Making mashed potato mounds for freezing

When boiling potatoes, cook extra, drain and mash with milk. Use an ice-cream scoop to make mounds of mashed potato on greased baking sheets, open-freeze them and transfer them to polythene bags. To use, place on a greased baking sheet, brush with beaten egg-and-milk, or melted butter, or top with grated cheese. Defrost and reheat at the same time in a moderately hot oven (200°C, 400°F, Gas Mark 6) for 25 minutes.

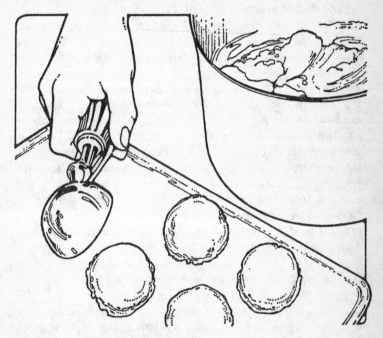

To fill a flan with frozen fruit

Instead of defrosting the fruit and flan case, arrange the fruit in the case while both are still frozen. Make up a jelly, or a jelly glaze (melted and sieved jam or fruit syrup thickened with arrowroot), pour it over the fruit and it will set almost at once. The fruit will remain plump and bright in colour.

Reheating frozen soups and sauces

Sometimes the defrosted food is too thin in consistency. It can be thickened in any of the following ways.

1 Measure 2 teaspoons cornflour for each 600 ml/1 pint liquid. Blend this with 2 tablespoons of the cold liquid and heat the remainder. Add the blended cornflour mixture, bring to the boil, stirring constantly, then stir over moderate heat for 2–3 minutes.

2 Bring the liquid to the boil. For each 600 ml/1 pint liquid blend 15 g/½ oz flour with an equal quantity of butter. Add this, in small pieces, to the pan and stir briskly until the mixture is smooth. Stir over moderate heat for 2–3 minutes.

3 For soups and sauces already thickened with egg or cream which should not be boiled, heat to boiling point, take off the heat and beat in an egg yolk to each 600 ml/1 pint liquid.

Freezing small portions for small families

It is often economical to cook in large quantities for freezing, but small families do not require, for instance, a whole cake or a terrine of pâté defrosted at one time. Bake a large cake, cool, cut in wedges and wrap individually in foil. If liked, reassemble into a round shape and over-wrap. Take out only as many portions as needed. The average thawing time is 1 hour, and slices of decorated cake will require to be open-frozen before packing and unwrapped before defrosting. Apply the same method to slices of pâté, and save small containers such as yogurt pots for sauces.

Allocating precious freezer space to home-grown vegetables

If there is a choice between allocating space to green or root home-grown vegetables, pack the green ones for freezing. Maincrop root vegetables will keep all winter if necessary in the earth and can be lifted and processed for freezing when stocks of green ones are partly used up.

Economizing on buying frozen vegetables

Buy large packs and re-pack them at home in meal-sized quantities. Or leave the vegetables in the large pack and pop in an empty yogurt pot so that you can easily scoop out an estimated quantity, allowing, for instance, that each person requires one pot full as a portion.

Making plate dinners for freezing

When preparing a roast dinner, cook extra potatoes, green vegetables and gravy. After the meal, make up one or two complete plate dinners for the freezer on partitioned foil plates, or foil plates saved from commercial products. There is really no extra work involved and the dinners come in handy when one member of the family has to eat alone.

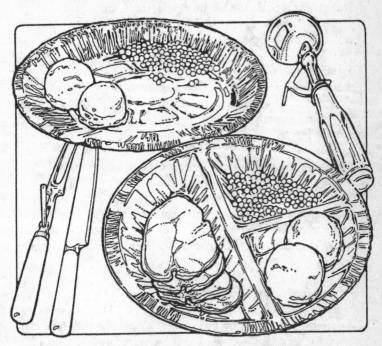

Time and fuel savers for reheating frozen dishes

If the time required to defrost and reheat in the oven is lengthy, it is often quite satisfactory to freeze the dish uncooked and add 10 minutes to the time indicated for defrosting and reheating in the oven to allow for cooking.

Fully exploiting a bulk buy of meat

You may be dismayed by the high proportion of apparent waste when meat is bought in bulk. Here is how to turn everything to good account.

1 Trim meat for packing or immediate transformation into cooked dishes. Cook all trimmings together with bones for stock.

2 Shred suet and keep for puddings.

3 Render down all other fat for dripping. Skim fat from cooked stock and add it to the dripping. If necessary, clarify dripping for long storage.

4 If the meat is pork, use the head and trotters for brawn.

5 If the meat is beef, ask the butcher to saw marrowbones in chunks and cook these.

To defrost meat slowly

Take the meat from the freezer and wrap the sealed pack in four sheets of newspaper to make a snug parcel. Leave at room temperature overnight or during the day and the meat will be defrosted but still cold.

To prevent metal freezing containers from sticking to shelves

Metal ice cube trays particularly seem to stick to the lining of the frozen food storage compartment. Before filling, rub the underside of such containers very lightly with glycerine; this will prevent them sticking to a frozen metal surface or to shelf grids.

Keeping freezer tape ready to use

Either turn in a narrow edge at the end of the tape to provide a handy tab to pull next time you need to use the roll, or slip a small button under the cut end to show where it is.

Saving space in the freezer for open-freezing

If space is limited and you want to open-freeze a number of trays of food like raspberries or French beans, keep a collection of small objects to place between baking trays to allow you to stack the greatest number possible in a small space. Ideal for the purpose are old-fashioned cotton reels, babies' building blocks and dumpy egg cups. Place one item from a set of four in each corner of a tray just the right height to allow another tray to be stacked on top and give clearance of the food being frozen.

How to work out your freezer running costs

Reckon that 1 unit of electricity is needed to run each 15 litres/ 0.5 cubic foot of storage capacity per week. To convert Imperial measures to metric measures for this, multiply the Imperial measurement by three and then add a nought.

To calculate actual food storage capacity of freezer

It should be possible to store about 10 kg/22 lb of food in each 30 litres/1 cubic foot of storage space. Remember, of course, that a light bulky food such as bread will need much more space than the same weight of a heavy compact food like meat, but on average the above calculation will give a reasonable guide to storage capacity.

Saving up for freezer supplies

If you find it hard to find sufficient funds for a bulk-buy at the freezer centre, keep a money box near the freezer and when you take out such items as a joint of meat, make a contribution to the box roughly equivalent to the cost of a similar joint from the butcher.

Getting the biggest crop from a small garden

Grow 'catch-crops' of lettuce and radishes between vegetables like onions and beetroot. (If the lettuces all ripen at once, use several lettuce hearts for a salad and make soup with the outer leaves.) Use decorative herbs like parsley as borders and place outdoor tomatoes among your flowers.

Growing plants without a garden

Many small vegetables and herbs can be grown in plant pots on a kitchen window sill. Not only parsley, mint and chives, but round lettuces grow well if planted singly in 10-cm/4-in pots, and if you have a little more room to spare a 25-cm/10-in pot will hold a tomato plant. Support tomatoes with sticks and feed them liquid plant food.

How to grow sprouting vegetables without soil

Have ready a large glass jar about 20 cm/8 in from base to neck. Place 15 g/½ oz alfalfa, or fenugreek, or 25 g/1 oz mung beans

59

in the jar. Cut a piece of muslin, stockinet or knitted nylon from tights to stretch over the neck of the jar and secure it in position with an elastic band. Fill the jar with warm water and drain through the cover several times. Place the jar on its side and shake until the plants make an even layer. Repeat the rinsing and draining process morning and evening until the sprouts are ready to eat. The growing time should be about 5 days.

Making fancy ice cubes

Use the strong plastic trays from chocolate boxes to make fancy-shaped ice cubes. Place on baking sheets to fill and freeze, otherwise the trays are too flexible to retain the water while it is freezing.

How to crush ice

Turn out a tray of cubes into the centre of a clean tea towel. Bring all four corners in together and twist until the 'neck' is as close to the ice as possible, then knock sharply against a hard surface. Or place the wrapped ice on a hard surface and hit it with a rolling pin.

Storing extra ice cubes

Make up a supply of ice cubes in trays and turn them out into a polythene bag before they begin to melt and stick together. Place the sealed bag in the freezer or freezing compartment of your refrigerator and refill the trays and freeze down another batch of cubes. Make as many bags of cubes as you will need for a party or during very hot weather and turn out one bag at a time as required.

Improvising ash trays for a party

Choose shallow dishes and fill them with sand to a depth of about 1.5 cm/½ in.

Making the most of candles

Place candles in the freezer for 3 hours before lighting to prevent uneven burning and unsightly 'tears' of wax. If the base of a candle is too small to sit securely in the holder, wrap a strip of tissue paper or foil round the base and press it firmly into the holder. If the base of the candle is too large, warm it and shave away sufficient wax with a sharp knife until it will fit.

Improvising a small vase
Pretty containers are often too light to hold flowers safely without tipping over. Fill the base with sand for safety's sake, which also makes it easier to arrange the flowers. A container that is cracked and slowly leaks water can still be used by pressing a beading of child's plasticine down the inside of the crack before filling the container with water.

Improvising a kitchen message pad
Keep a felt-tipped pen (the water-soluble kind) handy where you can write messages on a glazed tile surface. Writing can easily be removed by wiping with a damp cloth.

PART THREE

AN ALPHABET OF FOODS

There are all sorts of little snippets of information which help to make coping with food easier. This selection comprises a wealth of hints which I have noted as being useful in a really practical way. In fact they have been proved to work over and over again in my own kitchen.

Making bread

If you have time to make bread dough but not enough to attend to baking it immediately, put the unrisen dough in an oiled polythene bag, seal with a twist tie and put in the refrigerator. Cold retards the raising without killing the yeast, and the dough can be left overnight if necessary.

To use dried yeast

Double the quantity of fresh yeast if measuring by weight, but remember that 1 level tablespoon dried yeast granules is equivalent to about 25 g/1 oz fresh yeast. (The exact metric equivalent of 1 oz is 28.3 g.)

To make home-made bread which keeps fresh longer

Rub fat into the flour in the proportion of 25 g/1 oz fat for every 1.5 kg/3 lb 3 oz white flour or add 1 tablespoon malt extract to the same quantity of wholemeal flour.

To give a quick rise to bread dough

Alter the usual recipe in the following ways.

1 Use fresh yeast only (not dried yeast) and increase the quantity by half.

2 Add a 25-milligram vitamin C tablet dissolved in the yeast liquid per 0.75 kg/1½ lb flour.

3 Make up the dough in the usual way, turn out and knead for about 10 minutes. Cover with greased polythene and allow to rest for 5 minutes. Then divide into the required quantities and shape as desired.

To make bread with a crisp crust

Sieve the flour and warm it slightly. It is important to use warm water for mixing. To get the correct temperature without a thermometer, add 1 part boiling water to 2 parts cold water. Allow to rise in a warm place such as the airing cupboard and put a roasting tin of water on the floor of the oven while the bread is baking.

Giving bread a good finish

Add the following before or after baking.

1 Dissolve ½ teaspoon salt in 2 tablespoons water. Brush over

the bread and sprinkle with cracked wheat or poppy seeds before baking.

2 For a slight shine, rub baked bread with buttery paper.

3 For a plain glazed finish, beat 1 egg with 1 teaspoon water and use to brush the bread before baking.

4 For a soft crust, rub baked bread with buttery paper and cover with a cloth for 5–10 minutes.

5 For a sweet glazed finish, dissolve 1 tablespoon castor sugar in 1 tablespoon milk and use to brush baked enriched breads.

6 For a sticky glaze, brush baked enriched breads with warmed clear honey or golden syrup.

Calculating weights of risen dough

Twist off pieces of the risen and knocked-back dough as follows:

Small rolls – 50 g/2 oz
Large rolls – 75 g/3 oz
15-cm/6-in pizza base – 175 g/6 oz
20-cm/8-in pizza base – 225 g/8 oz
Small cob loaf – 350 g/12 oz
Large cob loaf – 0.75 kg/1½ lb
Small loaf (in 450-g/1-lb loaf tin) – 0.5 kg/1 lb 2 oz
Large loaf (in 1-kg/2-lb loaf tin) – 1 kg/2 lb 4 oz

To test that bread is cooked

Turn the loaf over and tap with your knuckles underneath. If cooked, it should sound hollow. If not quite ready, return to the oven without the tin and cook for a further 5 minutes.

To cut bread thinly without crumbling

When thin slices of bread are required for making fancy sandwiches, such as pinwheels, remove all crusts from an unsliced square loaf. Wrap the bread in a clean damp tea towel and allow to stand for 2 hours. The bread will then slice very thinly.

To freshen a stale loaf

Sprinkle or brush all over lightly with cold water. Place unwrapped in a hot oven (220°C, 425°F, Gas Mark 7) for 10 minutes. Rolls can be treated in the same way for 5 minutes only, or can be placed under a moderately hot grill, turning until crisp on both sides. Or, wrap the loaf of bread in a foil parcel and heat as above, then fold back the foil and return to the oven for a further 5 minutes to crisp the crust.

Using up crusts trimmed from bread

Melt some butter or margarine, dip the crusts in this to coat them, then toss in grated cheese spiced with garlic salt and paprika pepper or a hint of cayenne. Spread on a baking sheet and bake in a moderately hot oven until golden brown. Cool and store in an airtight container to serve with soups and salads.

Using up stale pieces of bread

If using the oven, spread odd pieces on a baking sheet and place in the coolest part until they are biscuit coloured. Break up and liquidize in a blender or roll between 2 sheets of grease-

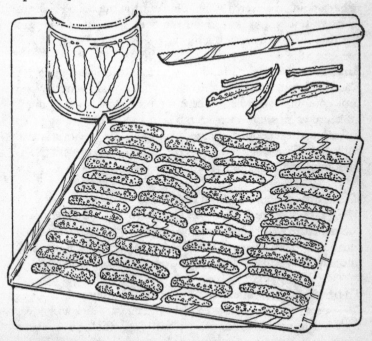

proof paper to the consistency of crumbs. When cold, store in a screw-topped jar or polythene bag. Use as a coating for fried foods, or combined with grated cheese for toppings.

Improvising a tea-time sweet with toast
Make a spread by combining 50 g/2 oz butter with the same weight of soft brown sugar, plus ½ teaspoon each of ground cinnamon and grated orange rind. Toast slices of white bread on both sides, spread with the mixture and place them under a hot grill until the mixture sizzles and forms a butterscotch topping. Serve cut into fingers.

To make melba toast
Buy sliced bread, fairly thick if possible, and keep it for several days as the toast is easier to make if the bread is not too fresh. Place the slices under a hot grill and brown them quickly on both sides. Split each slice in half through the soft centre using a sharp-pointed serrated knife. Dry out the uncooked sides of the toast under low heat, or in the oven if more convenient. The thin slices will curl attractively.

An easy way to make breadcrumbs for stuffing or sauce
Place the bread in a basin and cover with boiling water. When cool enough to handle, squeeze the bread to extract as much moisture as possible then crumble to use in the stuffing. To make bread sauce in the same way, place the bread in a pan with the milk, bring to the boil then mash until the mixture is smooth. Add flavourings as required.

Using frozen bread without defrosting
Always keep a cut loaf in the freezer so that you are never compelled to wait while a whole loaf thaws. Slices of frozen bread can easily be separated, quickly thawed under the grill, or completely toasted if required, from the frozen state.

To prevent crusts 'shelling off' home-baked bread
As soon as the bread is baked place it on a wire rack and cover with a slightly damp clean tea towel until cool. Or cool the bread in a steamy place such as a laundry room. This will

prevent the crust from becoming too dry in comparison with the moist inner crumb.

Substitutes for pastry tartlet cases
If you have no time to make pastry, cut small slices of bread square with the crusts trimmed off. Spread with softened butter and press each slice buttered side down into the centre of a bun tin so that the points stand up evenly. Bake in a moderately hot oven until golden brown but take care that the points do not become too brown. Allow to cool slightly and ease the cases carefully out of the bun tins.

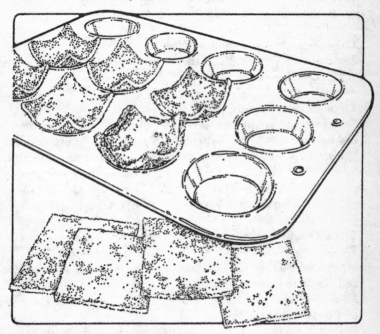

Substitute for dry breadcrumbs
If crisp crumbs are required, substitute finely crushed corn-flakes or other unsweetened cereal.

To prevent sandwich fillings discolouring bread
Use two thin slices of firm filling such as cheese or ham, instead of one thick slice for each sandwich. Then enclose soft

fillings like brown pickles, tomato sauce or chutney in the centre, keeping them away from the bread. This is particularly helpful if sandwiches are to be frozen or packed well in advance for picnics.

Making croûtons from sandwich trimmings

When you trim crusts from sandwiches, instead of throwing them away cut into small dice and fry in a mixture of butter and oil, dripping or chicken fat until crisp and golden brown. Drain well and use to serve with soup, or cool completely and store in the refrigerator for up to 7 days, or for up to 6 weeks in the freezer.

To make fancy sandwiches using sliced bread

Remove the crusts and roll the bread slice with a rolling pin until it is as thin as required.

To make rolled sandwiches

Cut the bread thinly with a knife dipped in hot water then shaken. Roll slices flat between sheets of greaseproof paper. Spread with butter creamed with the filling, roll up and then wrap tightly in sheets of foil. Pack close together in a polythene container or foil pack and chill. Slice each roll into thin sandwiches and they will keep their shape perfectly.

The do's and don'ts of cake making

Do ...

Make sure cake tins are dry and then grease them sufficiently and evenly to prevent sticking.

Measure quantities exactly because in the case of cake recipes they usually are critical.

Follow the recipe exactly when it comes to the size and shape of the tin. For example, using a smaller tin means that the mixture will be deeper and may take longer to cook, or may not cook successfully in the centre before the outside is burnt.

Don't ...

Over-mix cakes after you have added all the dry ingredients.

Open the oven door while a cake is baking if this can be avoided. But if it is essential, only open the door as far as is strictly necessary and close it gently. A rush of cold air drawn in by the escape of hot air automatically rising from the hot oven may cause cakes to sink.

To ensure that cake tins are evenly filled
Weigh one tin, fill with about half the cake mixture and note the weight. Replace with the other cake tin on the scales and fill with the remaining mixture, equalizing the weight of the two filled tins.

To ensure that cakes rise correctly
Only mix a cake containing a raising agent (baking powder, bicarbonate of soda, cream of tartar – or these ingredients combined in self-raising flour) when the oven is pre-heated to the correct temperature. The effect of the agent begins as soon as it comes in contact with liquid and if the mixture is kept waiting before baking it may not rise properly.

Adding flour to cake mixtures successfully
Avoid a streaky effect in the mixture by scraping down the sides of the bowl with a spatula during mixing. Do not fold in the flour in large quantities, otherwise there may be flour pockets in the baked cake. 'Tunnels' or large holes in a cake are caused by over-mixing when the flour is added. However, it is helpful to add 1 tablespoon of flour with the last addition of egg to prevent the mixture curdling at this stage.

To test that cakes are cooked
1 Sponge cakes and victoria sandwich mixtures – press the surface lightly in the centre with a fingertip. If it is firm and resilient to the touch, it is done.
2 Fruit cakes and teabreads – insert a fine skewer down to the base in the centre of the cake. If it comes out clean, the cake is done. Or use the old-fashioned test of listening carefully to the cake. If it is still audibly sizzling, it is not yet cooked.

How to make a neat Swiss roll
Turn the cake out of the tin on to a sheet of greaseproof paper or foil sprinkled with castor sugar. Trim the edges immediately with a sharp knife and roll up the cake from one end with the

paper inside. Allow to cool, unroll and spread with the filling. Re-roll, placing the join underneath.

To straighten a lop-sided sponge cake

Split the cake in half horizontally and turn the top layer until its thicker side is above the thinner side of the lower layer. Put together with a cream or buttercream filling rather than just jam so that you can make it absolutely level.

How to make small family-sized cakes

If a standard recipe requires a 20-cm/8-in tin, it is usually possible to double the quantities and divide the recipe between three 15-cm/6-in tins. The baking time will always require to be slightly reduced but you may find it more economical to have three smaller cakes than two large ones, when a whole cake tends to disappear at each meal.

One-stage mixing for a sandwich cake

Place equal weights of self-raising flour, soft margarine and castor sugar in a bowl. Add 1 teaspoon baking powder and 2 large eggs to each 100 g/4 oz flour. Beat with a wooden spoon until smooth for about 3 minutes, then bake in the usual way.

Cutting a sandwich cake in half neatly

Unless you have a long-bladed knife, this may be a tricky job. Try using a length of button thread in the same way as a cheese wire. Knot both ends of the thread through buttons so that you have something to pull against. For a crusty cake, you may need to use a cheese wire.

Making miniature cakes for children

Buy paper sweet cases or *petits four* cases and fill them with cake mixture. Bake in the usual way, reducing the cooking time by 2 or 3 minutes for the smaller quantities. Delicious and practical for babies and toddlers, and older children love them for dolls' tea parties.

To bake a Madeira cake

Do not put pieces of peel on the cake mixture before cooking. When nearly done, remove the cake from the oven, arrange thin slices of peel where the top shows signs of cracking and return to the oven for the last 10 minutes of cooking time.

Removing cakes from tins

Always leave cakes for 5 minutes in the tins to shrink before turning out. To avoid marking the delicate surface with the grid of the cake rack, turn out on to a clean tea towel on your hand and reverse on to the rack.

How to ice small fancy cakes quickly

Arrange the cakes on a wire rack and brush each one with a thin jam glaze. (This seals the loose surface of the cakes.) Place the wire rack over a sheet of foil or greaseproof paper. Spoon some icing over each cake in turn, then, starting with the first cake, guide the icing as it runs down the sides to cover completely. Remember to place decorations on the cakes before the icing sets fully. Small fairy cakes can be dipped into icing, holding the base of the cake firmly between thumb and forefinger. Turn upwards rapidly, before the icing begins to drip off.

How to coat the sides of a large cake

Spread the sides with buttercream or whipped cream. Either roll the cake in chopped nuts, chocolate vermicelli or toasted coconut spread on greaseproof paper, or place the cake on a rack over greaseproof paper and spoon the coating against the sides, using that which falls through the rack on to the paper for filling in spaces. Cover the top of the cake last of all.

Making a quick cake topping

Arrange a layer of halved marshmallows over the top and grill under moderate heat until they are lightly toasted. Or cover the top with chocolate peppermint creams, grill under a low heat until they begin to melt and mark into a pattern with the tines of a fork.

To prevent cake slices from crumbling

If a cake is very crumbly, take a plain biscuit cutter, dip in hot water, press it right through the centre of the cake then remove. Cut slices of cake up to this centre circle to avoid a crumbling edge.

To keep fruit cake moist

Store it in a tin with a quartered apple. If the cake is already dry, slice it and store in a sealed tin with the apple for 2 days before using.

How to make rock cakes which remain moist

Use 25 g/1 oz more fat than the recipe usually requires and sprinkle the tops of the cakes with demerara sugar before baking.

To retrieve a cake with a sunken centre

Use a sharp knife to remove a circle right down through the centre of the cake. This will leave a neat 'ring' cake ready for decoration.

Analysing why your cake went wrong

If the cake was made by the 'rubbed-in' method and had a heavy close texture, it might be for any one of the following reasons: too much flour, liquid or melted fat was used; your hands were too warm when rubbing in the fat; the mixture was over-beaten when the liquid was added. If the cake had a coarse, open texture, the fault may have been insufficient mixing, or using too hot an oven. (It is always advisable to keep fat at room temperature for 30 minutes before rubbing in to make it easier.)

If the cake was made by the 'creamed' method and had a heavy, close texture, it might be for any of the following reasons: insufficient creaming of fat and sugar; insufficient beating in of eggs; adding too much liquid; using too cool an oven. If the cake had a coarse, open texture, the fault may have been using too low a proportion of fat to sugar, or too high a proportion of flour to liquid.

How to make crisp shortbread

Instead of using all flour, substitute rice flour, cornflour or fine semolina for half the flour. This gives a crisper texture. Always mark shortbread lightly in fingers or wedges before baking to make it easier to cut when cooked.

Saving time shaping biscuits

Any biscuit mix which requires to be rolled out before using a biscuit cutter can be shaped into a large sausage, rolled in foil and chilled. Cut it in thin slices with a sharp knife before baking. The biscuit dough is easier to store uncooked until you have time to bake the biscuits and there are no wasted pieces which require re-rolling several times.

To make biscuit crumbs without mess

Place the biscuits in a large polythene bag and crush them with a rolling pin. You can see when the crumbs are fine enough. The same method applies to crushing potato crisps for coatings.

Making pastry with hard fat

If the fat is rather hard, use two round-bladed knives to cut it into the flour before rubbing in with the fingertips. If the fat is extremely hard or semi-frozen, grate it coarsely straight into the flour.

Rolling out pastry very thinly

Use a pastry cloth (a large square of thick canvas material). Cover the rolling pin with a 'sleeve' of narrow stockinet or with a clean nylon pop-sock. Fit one end of the rolling pin into the foot of the sock and secure the open end with an elastic band. Flour the pastry cloth and the sleeve very lightly and you can roll pastry as thin as you require without the dough sticking to either surface.

To lift very thin pastry

Roll out the pastry on greaseproof paper. Roll it up with the paper and then put it on a baking sheet or into a flan tin and unroll it in the other direction so that the pastry does not tear. Or roll the pastry lightly round the rolling pin and lift into place using the pin to support the weight, then turn the pin gently to unroll the pastry.

Lining fancy moulds with pastry

Roll out the pastry, lift it over the mould and ease it in to fit corners and fluted sides using a small ball of pastry. This stops the pastry from being punctured by the fingernails.

Trimming the top of a pastry-lined flan case

Ease the circle of pastry carefully into a fluted flan ring or flan tin. Press the pastry into the flutes with your knuckles or with a small ball of pastry as described above. To cut off the rough edges cleanly, pass the rolling pin across the top with one sharp stroke. The trimmings will fall away outside the flan case.

To prevent pastry in pies, tarts and flans becoming soggy

Bottom pastry

Line the baking tin and proceed as follows.

1 Brush the pastry with egg white then chill for 15 minutes before adding the filling to be cooked.

2 Spread the pastry with jam before adding a custard-type filling.

3 Bake the pastry case 'blind', then cool and add a filling which does not need to be cooked. Eat within 24 hours.

Top pastry
Cover the pie or tart with pastry, seal the edges well then slash
the top to allow steam from the filling to escape.

To identify the contents of pastry pies

As it is impossible to tell what the filling is from the outside,
prick out a few letters with a fine skewer on the pastry to
identify it. Or make letters instead of leaves from pastry trimmings, dampen and place on the pie before baking.

An easy lattice pie crust

Roll out the pastry to make a lid for the pie. Mark a design with
a skewer to give a lattice effect, allowing for the holes to be
evenly spaced. Dip a thimble or small bottle top in flour and
stamp out rows of small holes to your design. Lift carefully on
the rolling pin, place on the pie and seal the edges with milk or
beaten egg. This obviates the tiresome task of cutting and
weaving strips of pastry.

A short cut to making pastry patties

To make a number of small sweet or savoury patties with a prepared filling, you will need 450 g/1 lb shortcrust pastry. Roll out half thinly to line a greased baking sheet. Put spoonfuls of filling at regular intervals on top to make 12 patties. Brush round the fillings with egg wash (1 egg yolk plus 1 teaspoon water). Use the remaining pastry to make a cover and press down round the fillings. Brush with the remaining egg wash and cut into neat squares before baking.

Improvising baking beans

When a recipe requires a pastry case to be baked 'blind', you can use boiled and dried plum or peach stones, or small, smooth, clean pebbles instead of beans or rice on greaseproof paper. Make a collection of pebbles as nearly the same size as possible. Wash and dry carefully and store in a jar. They last indefinitely. Also, when a weight is required to fit exactly on top of a pâté tin or pudding basin, cover with foil and pour in your baking pebbles. If necessary, place a further heavy object on top of the pebbles.

To cook the underside of a double crust pie

While the oven preheats, put in a metal baking sheet. Put the pie plate on the hot baking sheet and the bottom will be cooked at the same time as the pastry crust.

To make puff pastry rise evenly

Roll out the pastry and cut into the required shapes. Place the pastry on dampened baking sheets and before baking, prick squares or oblong shapes in each corner with a large darning needle and prick circles at regular intervals all round the top edge.

Quick filling for vol-au-vent cases

Heat a 298-g/10½-oz can of undiluted condensed mushroom soup with 150 ml/¼ pint of single cream. Stir in 225 g/8 oz of finely-diced cooked chicken and place over a gentle heat, stirring carefully, until the chicken is hot. This quantity is sufficient to fill 24 6.5-cm/2-in vol-au-vent cases.

Making economy sausage rolls

Combine the sausagemeat with a made-up herb stuffing mix in the proportion of 1 kg/2 lb sausagemeat to one packet of stuffing mix. Use sage and onion or parsley and thyme.

Making economical savoury pastries

Instead of using grated cheese to make pastry straws, use finely crumbled square meat or chicken stock cubes instead. No additional seasoning is needed and they give interesting colour and flavour to savoury pastry titbits. Allow 2 crumbled cubes to 225 g/8 oz puff or flaky pastry.

Making bulk crumble and pastry mixes

If you often serve shortcrust pastry and crumble, make a large quantity of basic mix by rubbing fat into flour in the proportions of 1 to 2. This keeps well in a sealed container or a polythene bag in the refrigerator for up to six weeks, but even longer in the freezer. It requires the addition of cold water to make pastry, or an equal quantity of sugar to fat to make a crumble. The mix can even be used to make a whisked sauce by adding 75 g/3 oz mix to 600 ml/1 pint liquid in a saucepan and whisking over moderate heat until the sauce boils and thickens.

To make fluffy dumplings

Drop these into plenty of boiling water then bring back to simmering point only. When the dumplings rise to the surface pour 150 ml/¼ pint cold water over them, put a lid on the pan and continue simmering until the dumplings are cooked.

Using up left-over tea and coffee

Drain unsweetened black tea or coffee from the pot into a glass. A small amount of either (50 ml/2 fl oz per 600 ml/1 pint stock) adds interest to most meat dishes. Sweetened black tea can be used in meat dishes instead of cider. Serve chilled black tea with ice cubes, lemon, mint leaves and sugar if wished. Serve chilled black coffee with milk, cream or vanilla ice cream, sweetened if liked.

To make good tea

Have the pot warm and dry. Judge the amount of tea required according to the quality and strength of the tea, approximately 1 level teaspoon per cup. Take the pot to the kettle and pour on the water immediately it comes to the boil. Stir well and put on the lid. A fine leaf tea will take less time to draw than the large leaf teas. Pour the milk, if used, into the cups before the tea.

How to make good coffee without a special utensil

Use an earthenware or china jug. Put in 2 teaspoons of ground coffee per cup, and pour on the water just as it comes to the boil. Stir and leave for 3 minutes, then add 1 teaspoon of cold water per teaspoon of coffee. Stir well. Strain into cups and add milk or cream afterwards.

To make after-dinner coffee with granules

Make the coffee very slightly stronger than usual and add a tiny pinch of salt to each 600 ml/1 pint of coffee. This develops the flavour and the brew is almost indistinguishable from that made with ground coffee.

Interpreting descriptions of wines on labels

French: *brut* – extra dry, *sec* – dry, *demi-sec* – medium sweet, *doux* – sweet, *blanc* – white, *rouge* – red, *rosé* – pink, *mousseux* – sparkling, *pétillant* – semi-sparkling,
Italian: *secco* – dry, *abboccato* – sweet, *bianco* – white, *rosso* – red, *rosato* – pink, *spumante* –sparkling, *frizzante* – semi-sparkling.
German: *trocken* – dry, *süss* – sweet, *weiss* – white, *rot* – red, *rose* – pink, *sekt* – champagne, *schaumwein* – sparkling, *spritzig* – semi-sparkling,
Spanish: *seco* – dry, *dulce* – sweet, *bianco* – white, *tinto* – red, *rosado* – pink, *espumoso* – sparkling, *semi-espumoso* – semi-sparkling.

How to serve red wine at the correct temperature

The French term *chambré*, meaning room temperature, originated in times past when the dining room was rarely warmer than 16°C/60°F. In all cases, the wine will be sufficiently warm if it does not actually feel chilly to the touch when the hand is clasped round the bowl of the glass. Young robust wines benefit from being opened and allowed to 'breathe' for anything up to 24 hours before serving. More mature wines only require to be opened 2 hours before serving. All bottles of red wine should be placed upright for 48 hours before opening. Wines with a considerable amount of sediment are better decanted and then left to settle in case some sediment has been transferred to the decanter. If the wine is a fine old Burgundy, the decanter should be stoppered, as the wine will lose some of its bouquet by exposure to the air even for a short time.

Chilling wine quickly

If time permits, chill for two hours in the door of the refrigerator or for at least an hour lying horizontal in the refrigerator cabinet near the freezing compartment. If there are only minutes to spare, put the bottle in the freezer but do not leave it there for longer than 15 minutes. If forgotten, there is some risk of the bottle exploding as the wine will expand as it freezes. The fastest method of all and the one most suited to sparkling white wines is to stand the bottle upright in a container of crushed ice.

How to store left-overs of wine

If possible, transfer table wine to a clean bottle which it will almost fill. Re-corking a half-empty bottle allows sufficient air to come in contact with the wine to oxidize it and spoil the flavour. White and rosé wines can be kept, corked, in the refrigerator for two or three days. Add a teaspoon of brandy to red wine and it will keep at room temperature for up to a week. Or store left-over wine in the freezer, after which it will be suitable for cooking only. Do not mix wines, store them separately in polythene containers (not bottles with narrow necks) labelled according to colour.

To use up cider, fruit juice or flat lemonade

These liquids are useful for cooking pears, prunes or other dried fruit. Add to jellies in place of water, or to batter in place of milk. Use in stews instead of part of the stock or to make a good barbecue sauce.

Adding wine to give class to cooking

Very simple dishes are easily elevated to *haute cuisine* standard by using a little wine. A simple béchamel sauce to serve over fish or vegetables is improved by adding white wine to the milk, or by adding a few tablespoons of reduced wine to the complete sauce. Add reduced wine also to cheese sauces, rarebits, batters; even poach eggs in it!

How to use wine in cooking

The cooking process is intended to evaporate the alcohol content of the wine while retaining the flavour. Either add wine to the dish at the beginning (such as at the start of a casserole dish), or use it for basting during roasting. If it must be added near the end of cooking, reduce the wine by boiling it to half the original quantity, preferably in a shallow pan to hasten evaporation, then it can be added to the dish even at the last moment.

Assessing the contents of wine glasses for cooking

Many recipes suggest adding a glass of table wine without specifying an exact quantity. Capacities vary according to the shape of the glass, from 125 ml/4 fl oz to 250 ml/8 fl oz. The universally-used Paris goblet holds 150 ml/5 fl oz ($\frac{1}{4}$ pint). That would therefore be the average amount. Fortified wines (such as sherry and Marsala) influence a dish without being used in such a large quantity.

To sour milk for cooking

Stir 1 tablespoon lemon juice or vinegar into 300 ml/$\frac{1}{2}$ pint milk and allow to stand at room temperature until thickened.

Saving money on milk for baking

You can economize by using reconstituted dried milk (which is indistiguishable from fresh milk in baking). For a slimming diet, use reconstituted, dried, low fat skimmed milk. If your aim is to avoid using animal fat, use the dried milk which has had animal fat extracted and vegetable fat substituted.

Making butter milk cheaply at home

It is necessary to use a small quantity of commercial buttermilk as a starter. Make up 450 ml/¾ pint of dry skimmed milk with dry powder and water to mix. Place in 600 ml/1 pint polythene container and add 150 ml/¼ pint commercial buttermilk and a pinch of salt. Mix lightly, cover and allow to stand at room temperature overnight. Next day, stir well and chill. Reserve a little of this buttermilk to 'start' your next batch but invest in a new commercial pot every sixth batch.

Making yogurt cheaply at home

Make sure that all utensils are absolutely clean – cleansing them in a sterilizing solution if possible. It is necessary to use a small quantity of commercial natural yogurt as a starter. Warm 600 ml/1 pint UHT (long life) milk to blood heat. Remove from the heat. Lightly whisk in 150 ml/¼ pint natural yogurt and pour the mixture into a thermos flask. Seal and allow to stand overnight. Next day pour into small containers, add fruit juice or pieces of fruit to flavour if liked and chill until set. Reserve a little of the plain yogurt to 'start' your next batch but buy a fresh commercial supply every sixth batch.

Substitute for cream in sauces

Natural yogurt can often be used instead of single cream. It is cheaper and less fattening and the flavour is slightly stronger than that of cream.

To whip evaporated milk

Chill the can. Open, pour out the contents, add 1–2 teaspoons lemon juice per large can and whisk until thick.

To sour fresh cream

Add 1 teaspoon lemon juice to 150 ml/¼ pint single cream, stir well and allow to stand for 30 minutes before using.

To extend double cream

Stiffly whisk 1 egg white with 2 teaspoons castor sugar. Whip 150 ml/¼ pint double cream until thick and fold in the meringue which will almost double the quantity. To make a Crème Chantilly, add a few drops of vanilla essence to the whipped cream before adding the meringue.

Removing salt from butter for cooking

Some recipes require unsalted butter and if you only have salted butter in stock, melt 100 g/4 oz in 300 ml/½ pint warm water, stir well, then allow to set. When completely cold, drain off the salty water and the butter is ready to use.

To soften butter quickly

1 To cream butter for easy spreading, add a teaspoon of very hot water to 50 g/2 oz butter and work in with a fork.

2 To soften butter for creaming, rinse out the mixing bowl with very hot water and add the cubed butter with the sugar on top. Beat with a fork.

3 To soften butter by microwave for creaming, place with the sugar in a suitable mixing bowl and microwave for 15 seconds.

To make successful butter curls

Have ready a bowl of iced water into which you can drop the completed butter curls, and a second bowl in which you can dip the curler. The block of butter should be at room temperature. Pull the curler along the top surface of the butter from one end to the other and shake off the curl which forms into the iced water. Do not touch the curls with your warm fingers. When the curls are required, lift out one at a time with a skewer, allow to drain and pile up in a butter dish.

To clarify butter or margarine

Melt the fat then continue heating over gentle heat until no more bubbles rise to the surface. Do not allow the fat to turn golden. Remove from the heat and leave to stand for 5 minutes, then pour off the clean fat leaving the sediment behind.

Economizing on butter in cooking

Fat rendered down from pork and beef trimmings can be used in fruit cakes, pastry, and especially in suet crust. Clarify the fat by bringing it to the boil in plenty of water, then allow to cool until the fat forms a solid cake. Remove carefully with a slotted draining spoon and scrape impurities away from the underside of the fat with a round-bladed knife. Reheat until no more bubbles form then pour into a clean dry basin and allow to set.

To heat butter without burning

Always add at least 1 teaspoon of oil to each 25 g/1 oz butter. This addition has two effects – since butter contains a proportion of water, it reduces the percentage of water in the mixture as a whole, thus reducing dangerous spluttering; and since oil can be heated to a much higher temperature than butter before it begins to burn, it raises the temperature at which the combined fat and oil starts to turn brown.

Keeping cheese fresh

Cheese in an enclosed dish easily becomes mouldy. To prevent this, place a sugar lump on the cheese in the dish.

To give a fondue a creamy texture

When the fondue is ready for serving, stir in a little unwhipped whipping cream. Four tablespoons should be sufficient for a fondue to serve four people.

To correct a cheese fondue which has separated

Gradually add up to 1 tablespoon vinegar and stir in a figure-of-eight shape until the fondue returns to its smooth, creamy consistency.

To use up left-over cheese

Blue cheeses are best but any strong-flavoured cheese will do for potting. Grate up the cheese and pound it into the same weight of softened butter. Continue pounding, gradually adding 1 tablespoon of brandy or dry sherry for each 100 g/4 oz of cheese. Seasoning such as a teaspoon of mustard may be added to taste. Press into a small pot and cover with a thin layer of melted butter.

To set a jelly quickly

Dissolve the jelly cubes in a small amount of boiling water then add ice cubes to the required level, stirring constantly to ensure that they dissolve before the jelly sets. Or put the jelly cubes in a suitable measuring jug with a little water to cover and microwave for 1 minute. Stir and microwave for a further 3 seconds if necessary. When completely dissolved, add the remaining water or ice cubes as above.

To increase the volume of jelly

When it is syrupy but not quite set, whisk the jelly vigorously to incorporate as much air as possible. The texture will be spongy and the jelly almost doubled in volume.

How to turn out a moulded mousse or jelly

It is necessary to release the seal between the mould and the food. To do this, press the surface of the food with the finger-tips to pull it away from the sides of the mould all round. Dip the mould into hot water for just a few seconds, then invert it over a damp serving dish and shake gently until the food drops out on to the dish. Because the surface of the dish is damp, it is possible to centre the food quite easily by sliding it into position.

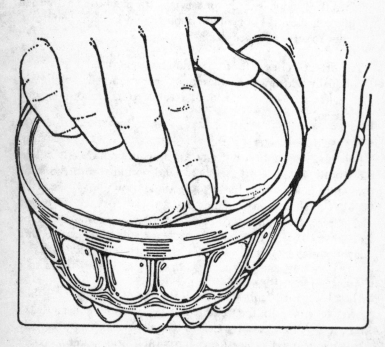

To use a moulded jelly which has collapsed

Place the jelly in a basin and whip it up with a fork. Serve piled up in glass dishes.

Short cut to making peach melba

Arrange drained canned peach halves over vanilla ice cream. Melt 1 tablespoon raspberry jam with 1 tablespoon syrup from the can for each portion, and sieve over the peach halves.

Steaming puddings economically

Use a large saucepan and add potatoes or other vegetables to the boiling water. Make sure you are boiling the pudding in a polythene, ovenproof glass or china basin – don't use metal.

To slow down the cooking time of a milk pudding

If you wish to leave a complete meal cooking in the oven and the main dish needs a longer cooking time than the pudding, prepare the meal in the usual way but place the rice mixture in a heavy ovenproof glass dish and cover with a sheet of foil with shiny side outwards. Crimp the edges well under the rim of the dish and place it in the coolest part of the oven. The pudding will take at least 30 minutes longer than usual to cook but there will be less risk of it becoming overcooked.

To make a delicious crust on milk puddings

Add 150 ml/$\frac{1}{4}$ pint evaporated milk to each pint of fresh milk and pour a few spoonfuls of evaporated milk on top of the pudding half-way through baking time. Or use ordinary milk and stir in the crust twice during baking time, pouring several spoonfuls of single cream on top of the pudding after the last stirring.

To test whether egg whites are beaten stiffly enough

Tilt the basin gradually until it is completely inverted. If they are stiff enough, the whites will not fall out. If they begin to slide as you tilt the basin, continue whisking.

Whisking egg whites successfully

First ensure that there is not even a particle of egg yolk in the whites, that the whisk is absolutely clean and dry and that there is no moisture or grease in the bowl. The eggs should be at room temperature before being cracked. Whisk the whites until they stand in glossy peaks, you should be able to turn the bowl upside down without the egg whites sliding about (see above). Do not over-whip, as if whipped to the dry stage the whites become granular and will not incorporate easily into any other mixture. For meringues, add half the measured sugar and whisk until the mixture stands in firm shiny peaks. Fold in the remaining sugar with a metal tablespoon.

Storing eggs in the frozen state

When you have a surplus of eggs in the kitchen or they are low in price, freeze them in small quantities so that you need only use one or two eggs at a time, as required. Beat the eggs allowing 1 teaspoonful salt or 1½ teaspoonfuls sugar per 5 eggs as a stabilizer. Have ready a number of plastic tub lids. Pour 2 tablespoons of the egg mixture into each, open-freeze, remove when solid and pack with dividers of foil, freezer tissue, or polythene. Each little block is equivalent to one egg.

To enrich and thicken sauces with egg yolks

When a sauce is fully cooked the addition of an egg yolk further thickens it and gives a beautiful gloss. Never add the egg yolk to the pan; add a little hot sauce to the yolk in a cup or small basin, beating well all the time. Stir the mixture into the sauce, removing it at once from the heat. Do not allow the sauce to boil or it may curdle. If cream is to be added to the sauce at the end of cooking time, beat the egg yolk and cream together and incorporate them as above.

Ways to separate an egg

1 If you have a steady hand, hold the egg and rap it sharply in the centre against the rim of a mixing bowl or cup. As you do this, move your hand slightly in over the bowl or cup so that none of the white is wasted. Using both hands, gradually separate the shell into two halves, cradling the yolk in one half. Tip the yolk into the other half allowing the white to fall into the container and repeat the process until the yolk has no more white clinging to it. With practice you can acquire the chef's tip of jamming the half containing the yolk into the other half at an angle so that you can put this down on a working surface as a temporary container.

2 Break the egg on to a saucer or small plate. Invert an egg cup over the yolk with one hand and with the other pick up the saucer and allow the egg white to drain from it into a bowl, making sure that you keep the egg cup pressed tightly against the surface.

3 Break the egg on to a saucer or small plate as above. Using a rounded soup spoon carefully scoop up the yolk and remove.

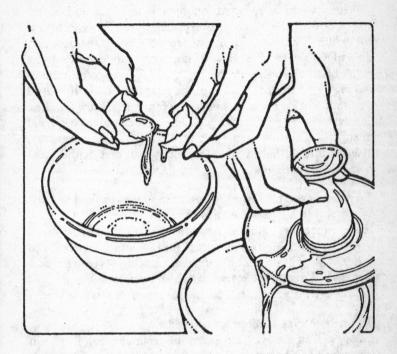

Ways to use left-over egg yolks

1 Add to omelette mixtures, pancakes or scrambled eggs to enrich them.

2 Use as egg wash, mixed with a little cold water, to glaze pastry or bread.

3 Make classic mayonnaise with egg yolks rather than with whole eggs.

4 Beat into mashed potato to transform it into *pommes duchesse.*

Ways to use left-over egg whites

1 Use to make meringues or macaroons.
2 Whisk and add to sweetened whipped cream to transform it into Crème Chantilly.
3 Whisk and fold into a jelly which is on the point of setting to increase the volume.

How to make a one-egg meringue

One egg white is so often left over in cooking and is not sufficient to make a conventional meringue recipe. Put your egg white in a bowl with 6 rounded tablespoons castor sugar, 1 teaspoon white vinegar, 2 tablespoons boiling water and a pinch of salt. Whisk over boiling water for about 10 minutes (taking an occasional rest) until the mixture is quite stiff. Add 1 teaspoon baking powder and whisk for a further few minutes. (The process is much quicker if you can use an electric hand mixer.) Dry the meringue out in the oven in the usual way. The mixture is slightly more powdery than that of the usual home-made meringue.

To prevent scrambled eggs becoming over-cooked

When you judge that the eggs have reached exactly the right stage, either serve immediately on to warm plates, or arrest cooking by dipping the bottom of the pan into a bowl of cold water. This will prevent any further cooking by contact with the residual heat in the pan itself, which quickly makes the eggs too set even if you switch off the source of heat immediately.

To retrieve over-cooked scrambled eggs

Drain well in a sieve then place the scrambled egg in a basin over a pan of hot water. Mash with a fork and blend in a little cream or top-of-the-milk until the mixture is creamy. Add seasoning and serve when piping hot.

To boil a cracked egg safely

Mould the egg closely in foil and allow at least 1 minute longer than usual for cooking.

Economy egg wash

When only a small amount of egg wash is required, use the

yolk of one egg with 1 tablespoon of water or milk and if liked add a pinch of salt or sugar according to whether savoury or sweet flavouring is required. Freeze the left-over egg white for use in future cooking, such as for making a meringue or mousse.

Making meringues

Whisk the egg whites until really stiff and add cream of tartar or cornflour in the proportion of $\frac{1}{4}$ teaspoon to each 3 egg whites, with half the sugar. Whisk again until the mixture stands in stiff glossy peaks then fold in the remaining sugar with a metal spoon. This method should ensure that no sugar syrup oozes from the meringues during cooking.

To bake a meringue flan case successfully

Line a baking sheet with foil, shiny side upwards, or with non-stick cooking parchment. Pipe the meringue mixture directly on to this surface and bake in the usual way. When the meringue case is cooked, it will lift from the liner without any difficulty. If very delicate, allow to become cold then peel the liner gently away from underneath.

To retrieve a meringue round which has cracked

Stick the pieces together with whipped cream to give the meringue its original shape. Decorate the top with grated chocolate or sifted icing sugar to disguise the cracks.

To make lighter pancakes, waffles or fritters

Use your normal recipe for the batter but beat the egg yolks only into the flour with the milk or milk liquid. Allow the batter to stand in the usual way and just before frying, stiffly whisk the egg whites and fold them in. (The finished batter will be lighter in texture and will go further when cooked.)

To turn out an omelette successfully

As soon as the omelette is cooked, remove from the heat. Tilt the pan away from you and fold the omelette over quickly to form a half circle. Holding a warm plate in the right hand, and with the left hand underneath the handle of the omelette pan, tilt the two towards each other and gently but quickly slip the omelette over on to the plate and serve immediately.

Preparing a soufflé in advance

The basic mixture for a soufflé may be prepared well in advance, leaving only the whisked egg whites to be added just before cooking time commences. Make sure, however, that the oven is preheated to the required temperature.

To prevent discoloration of hard-boiled egg whites

Immediately the cooking time is over, pour off the boiling water from the saucepan and replace it with cold water. Allow the eggs to stand for 5 minutes before shelling.

To test the freshness of an egg

Break the egg on to a plate. The yolk should float intact on the thick, firm white. If the egg is not fresh the white spreads thinly and the egg yolk has a tendency to break. If the egg is to be cooked in the shell, drop it gently into a glass of water. A fresh egg will sink to the bottom on its side. A not-so-fresh egg will rise from the bottom and tilt to a more vertical position.

To make a good pancake batter

For delicate, paper-thin, lacy pancakes, the batter should be the consistency of thin cream so that it spreads easily over the base of the pan. The additional of a tablespoon of oil beaten in at the last moment improves the texture and economizes on the amount of fat required for frying.

To test the temperature of fat for deep-frying without a thermometer

Heat the fat then drop in a 2.5-cm/1-in cube of bread. If the bread turns golden brown in 20 seconds the temperature is approximately 195°c/385°F, if it takes 40 seconds the temperature is approximately 190°C/375°F, if it takes 1 minute the temperature is approximately 176°C/350°F.

Coating foods for frying

Place the coating (seasoned flour, rolled oats, breadcrumbs, chopped nuts) in a polythene bag. Add the food to be coated and shake gently, holding the bag closed. Remove the coated items on to a clean dry surface until all are prepared for cooking.

To make a batter coating adhere for frying

Ensure that the food to be coated is dry and if necessary turn lightly in flour before coating. If the food is moist, steam forms during cooking and forces the batter away from the food. Also, check that the temperature of the cooking fat or oil is sufficiently high before putting in the food and do not add too many items at one time, thus lowering the temperature.

To make crisp batter coating for food

Substitute cornflour for part of the flour, in the proportion of one-third cornflour to two-thirds flour by weight.

To drain oily foods without soft kitchen paper

Crumple some foil and lay the cooked pieces of food on it. The excess fat will run down into the creases.

Frying without fat

A teflon-coated or silverstone non-stick pan makes this relatively easy. Even eggs can be successfully dry-fried if you use an implement for lifting made of nylon, plastic or wood, instead of a metal fish slice which could damage the pan lining.

To remove smells from oil or fat used for deep-frying

Place the oil or fat in a pan and heat until warm. Add slices of raw potato and continue heating until the potato is golden brown. Remove the potato, strain the oil or fat, then cool.

To make a crisper coating for fried food

Roll cornflakes between two layers of greaseproof paper until they become as fine as breadcrumbs. Use them to coat foods for frying exactly as you would breadcrumbs. Any unsweetened cereal can be used for coating if finely crushed.

Using up duck fat

Most sauces for duck are very rich and rely mainly on the juices from the duck and giblet stock. Surplus fat skimmed from the roasting tin is very well flavoured and ideal for frying croûtons, making pâté, spreading on hot toast, or enriching a stew.

Buying fish

Whether it has been frozen or not before arriving on the fish-monger's slab, fish should smell perfectly fresh without any trace of an ammoniac odour. The flesh should be firm and should not retain the imprint of the fingers when handled; the eyes should be red and the scales silvery.

Filleting fish

Cut through the skin and flesh closely along one side of the backbone. Raise the fillet away from the bone from the centre to the side, holding with one hand and cutting with the other, working from the head to the tail. Turn the fish round and remove the other fillet in the same way. Turn it over and remove the other two fillets from the backbone. If the fish is small and only two fillets are required, begin from the head end where the fish has been gutted, slip the knife in just above the bone and ease the whole fillet away towards the tail. Turn the fish over and remove the other fillet. Always work from head to tail and away from yourself when filleting.

1   2

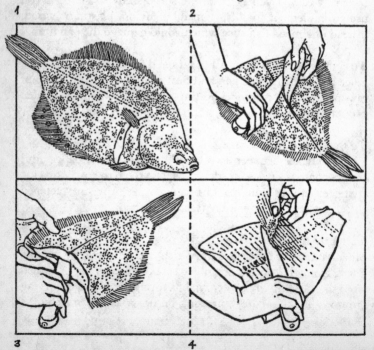

3   4

Skinning frozen fish fillets
Place frozen fillets in cold water for 5 seconds. You can then rip the skin from the flesh without damage, leaving the fillets whole and still frozen stiff.

Skinning a fresh fish fillet
Dip the fingers of one hand in salt to get a good grip, and hold the tail end of the fillet, skin side downwards, on a board. Using a straight-bladed knife, slice the flesh away from the skin, starting close to your fingers and working away from yourself.

Removing scales from whole fresh fish
Place the fish on an old clean board and drive a nail through the tail to secure it. Make a scraper by nailing two or three beer bottle caps to a small block of wood and use this to remove the scales, working from the tail towards the head on both sides of the fish. With a little practise you can remove the fish scales without damaging the fish skin or the flesh.

To fry fish fillets
Always place in fat hot enough to sizzle immediately, skin side uppermost. This prevents the fillet from curling and ensures a good colour. If the fat is slightly burnt or contains pieces of the coating by the time you turn the fillets over, the resultant discoloration will not be noticeable as it will occur on the skin side. Test the fish with a fork – if it is cooked the flesh will break into firm flakes.

Cooking fish with minimum smell
Dot with butter and sprinkle with seasoning. Steam in a soup plate covered with a close-fitting lid or a heatproof glass plate over a saucepan of boiling water such as one in which potatoes are boiling. Prepare a roux, add sufficient milk to make a thick sauce, then strain in the juices from cooking the fish. To finish the sauce, stir in seasoning, capers, lemon juice, or chopped parsley and keep the fish covered until the sauce is ready.

Keeping fish whole during poaching in a fish kettle
Place the fish on a piece of cheesecloth or muslin and tie a knot in each end so that the fish lies in a hammock. Hold the knotted

ends to lower the fish into the poaching liquid and to remove for draining after cooking.

Cooking large whole fish without a fish kettle

If you have no fish kettle, wrap the prepared fish to make a well-sealed foil parcel. Place diagonally in a roasting tin and pour 150 ml/¼ pint boiling water into the tin. Place in a moderately hot oven (190°C, 375°F, Gas Mark 5) for 15 minutes per 450 g/1 lb up to 1.5 kg/3 lb in weight and thereafter 10 minutes per 450 g/1 lb. Lift out carefully on to a board and open the parcel at once if it is to be served hot. To serve cold, allow the fish to cool in the foil parcel to keep the flesh moist and juicy.

To make a court bouillon for cooking fish

Place 600 ml/1 pint water and half that quantity of white wine in a large pan. Add 1 medium onion and 1 medium carrot, sliced, 1 bouquet garni, 1 teaspoon salt and 4 white peppercorns. Bring to the boil, cover and simmer for 20 minutes. Strain, and use to cook delicately flavoured fish or shellfish. When cooking strongly-flavoured or oily fish, substitute vinegar for half the quantity of wine.

To make a stronger stock for cooking fish

Make the stock as above, but add the head, bones and trimmings from the fish to the pan before cooking it. Also, use rosé or red wine instead of white wine if available. This richer stock is particularly suitable for cooking salmon.

Shelling prawns and shrimps

Start peeling the body shell where it joins the head and when it is detached from the flesh, pinch the tail to squeeze out the flesh. The shell should then lift off to leave the body intact. Twist the head to remove it. If preferred, de-vein the shellfish after shelling by removing the vein down the back with the tip of a skewer or a pointed knife.

To remove a fishy smell from hands or cutlery

Rub over with the cut surface of a lemon then wash and rinse well.

To make salty pickled herrings edible

Pour boiling water over the fish, then drain. Repeat the process several times if necessary to remove excess salt. Cool, and if still too salty, chop and combine with chopped dessert apple and whipped cream.

To prevent brown sugar from hardening

Store in an airtight container, preferably in the freezer. It can be spooned out of the container in the frozen state.

How to soften brown sugar which has hardened

Place it in a bowl, cover with a clean damp cloth and leave for several hours. Or microwave it for 30 seconds then break it up with a fork and repeat if necessary.

To produce fine sugars cheaply

Use your blender to reduce granulated sugar to the consistency of either castor or icing sugar. The price of granulated sugar is less than that of finer sugars.

To make vanilla sugar

Place 450 g/1 lb castor sugar in a polythene container. Push a vanilla bean into the sugar, seal the container and leave it for 3 weeks, shaking it occasionally. The bean can then be rinsed, dried and used again. If you want a particularly fast result, split the bean lengthways and push both pieces into the sugar. The flavoured sugar will then be ready in 10 days but the pieces of bean cannot be re-used. When substituted in place of ordinary sugar, vanilla sugar imparts a lovely flavour to egg custards and other delicate desserts.

Economy hint on using sugar substitutes

Sugar used to sweeten drinks costs relatively more than artificial sweeteners and may cause a weight problem as well. Buy a big dispenser of sweeteners and keep it near the tea-making apparatus.

To make a paper piping bag for icing

Take a piece of greaseproof paper 25 cm/10 in square and cut it in half to make two triangles. Lay one triangle on a flat surface, with the long side towards you. Take the point on the right-hand side, roll it under once and place it on top of the right-angled corner pointing away from you. Take the left-hand point and bring it round the bag, placing it under the right-angled corner. Holding all three points together, fold down the edge of the bag two or three times to make a collar and keep the bag together. Place a little icing or butter cream in the bag and snip a small piece off the point. The smaller the snip, the finer the flow of icing will be.

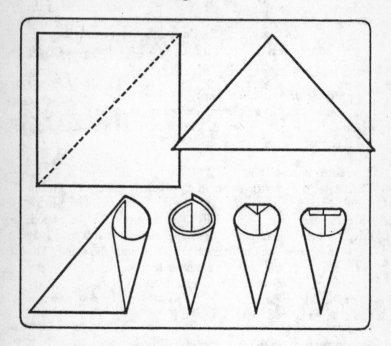

To prevent icing from hardening

Add 1 teaspoon glycerine to each 450 g/1 lb icing sugar when making royal icing or moulded icing.

To soften icing made up in advance

Place it in a basin over a pan of hot water and work it until soft enough to use, or place it in a suitable basin, cover and microwave for 15 seconds.

How to melt chocolate
Put it in a basin over hot, not boiling, water. If chocolate is over-heated, the cocoa butter separates out and goes grey and crumbly, spoiling the shine and smooth texture.

Making chocolate shapes for decorations
Draw or trace off required shapes on white paper and cover with a sheet of non-stick cooking parchment (or draw directly on to the parchment). Fill a greaseproof paper piping bag with melted chocolate, snip off the end and pipe in the outline of the shape. Spoon melted chocolate into the centre if a solid shape is required, or pipe lines within the outline. When the shapes are completely set, peel off the paper lining carefully. The melted chocolate is inclined to harden quickly in the piping bag. If necessary, heat it in a basin over hot water to soften again.

Avoiding waste when melting chocolate
Break the chocolate into a basin and melt it over hot water in the usual way. Scrape out as much as possible and then place the basin in the refrigerator or freezer until the remaining chocolate hardens. Scrape out with a metal spoon to make chocolate chips for decorating ice-cream or desserts.

To give a strong chocolate flavour
Use cocoa powder instead of melted chocolate in cooking. Either combine the dry cocoa powder with the flour or add it with the liquid, mixing it to a paste first with a little boiling water. Use in the proportion of half the weight of cocoa powder to melted chocolate but remember to add a little extra sugar because cocoa powder is unsweetened. A small amount of coffee essence or instant coffee strengthens chocolate flavour.

Adding artificial food colourings and flavourings
As this is a difficult job to gauge accurately and most flavourings are highly concentrated, add cautiously and in the case of colourings only add a few drops at a time. If the bottle has no dropper, use a clean medicine dropper, or add from the tip of a skewer or a steel knitting needle. If you add too much colour-

ing or flavouring, make up more basic mixture and gradually combine part of the first batch until a satisfactory result is obtained. If this is impossible, try to conceal the error. For example, if gooseberry fool is coloured too dark a green, pipe or swirl the surface with whipped cream.

How to use candied angelica

Soak a piece of angelica in hot water until it softens and becomes flexible. Drain, and pat dry on soft kitchen paper. To make diamonds, cut into wide strips lengthways and then in parallel lines diagonally into diamond shapes. To make handles for fancy cakes, cut very thin strips and bend in the centre to form hoops.

An economical substitute for preserved ginger

Peel a marrow, remove the seeds and cut it into small cubes. Weigh 450 g/1 lb marrow cubes. Measure an equal quantity of granulated sugar, and 25 g/1 oz ground ginger. Keep these to one side. Place the marrow cubes in a preserving pan and add just sufficient water to cover. Stir in the sugar and ginger and bring slowly to the boil, stirring, then simmer without stirring until the cubes become transparent. Remove the marrow cubes from the syrup with a slotted draining spoon and place in a bowl. Reduce the remaining syrup in the pan by rapid boiling until it measures 300 ml/½ pint. Add a further 450 g/1 lb granulated sugar and 50 g/2 oz ground ginger. Stir over low heat until the sugar has completely dissolved, then allow to boil for 5 minutes. Pack the 'ginger' cubes into warm jars, fill up with the syrup and seal while still hot. Allow to mature for 1 week before using.

How to use gelatine successfully

Leaf gelatine, sometimes suggested in older recipes, requires to be washed, then soaked in cold water until soft, which takes about 25 minutes. Then it may be used as the powdered variety. Three leaves of gelatine are equivalent to a 15-g/½-oz sachet of powdered gelatine, or 1 tablespoon. The most successful way to use it in a recipe is to add water in the proportion of 2 tablespoons cold water to 1 tablespoon gelatine in a basin and allow it to stand for about 5 minutes to soften. Place the basin over a pan of hot water for about a further 5 minutes until it is completely dissolved. The liquid will be transparent with no granules visible. Allow it to cool slightly, then whisk or stir it briskly into the mixture to be set. This avoids ropy threads of set gelatine spoiling the texture. (If the dissolved gelatine becomes cold and set before adding it to the food, replace it over hot water until it has melted.)

Making an economical almond paste
Substitute some fine semolina for part of the ground almonds in the proportion of 1 part semolina to 3 parts ground almonds. Or substitute soya flour for part of the ground almonds in the same proportions as above. Use extra almond essence and lemon juice to give a stronger flavour.

To prevent tomato purée giving a bitter taste in cooking
When using tomato purée, add sugar in the proportion of 1 teaspoon sugar to each 2 tablespoons tomato purée. Stir this into the mixture and allow to cook for at least 5 minutes. The addition of sugar in these proportions does not impart a sweet taste, it simply removes the bitterness which sometimes results from using very concentrated tomato purée.

Freezing grapes as a year-round garnish
When small seedless white grapes are in season, freeze some small packs without added sugar or syrup, each containing sufficient to use as a garnish for hot fish dishes, cold chicken, made-up turkey dishes, etc. They keep their shape and texture well and add a pretty touch of colour to creamy-looking food.

Topping and tailing fruit quickly
Gooseberries and all kinds of currants are quite tiresome to 'top and tail'. Open-freeze the fruit, pack it into polythene containers, and when you require to use it, shake the container sharply several times. Some of the stems and flower-ends will break off immediately and the others are easy to break off while the fruit is still frozen. You need not use scissors.

Saving citrus fruit rinds

When peeling citrus fruit (oranges, grapefruits, lemons, limes, satsumas):

1 Grate the bright, oily, outer rind, mix it with castor sugar and store it in an airtight pack or container in the refrigerator or freezer. It is useful for topping uncooked cake mixtures or ice-cream.

2 Pare thin strips of rind, or scrape the white pith from larger pieces of rind, and cut it into shreds. Boil for a few minutes until soft, drain well and use the water to make a heavy sugar syrup (225 g/8 oz sugar to 300 ml/½ pint liquid). Stir in the shreds of peel and store the syrup in screw-topped containers in the refrigerator or freezer – it is useful for topping steamed or baked puddings.

For other uses for citrus fruit peel see page 45.

To obtain the maximum juice from citrus fruit

Place one fruit at a time in the microwave oven for 30 seconds before squeezing out the juice.

To make a lemon tie

Take half a lemon and cut a slice from the pointed end so that it will sit firmly on a plate with the larger cut side uppermost. Pare a sliver of rind about 0.5 cm/¼ in deep round the cut surface of the lemon leaving about 1.5 cm/½ in attached. Tie the long end into a single knot and use the lemon half to garnish fish dishes.

Keeping a stock of lemon slices

Lemon halves often shrivel up in the refrigerator unused. Slice them while still fresh, open-freeze so that they will not stick together, then pack them in bags and store in the freezer. They are handy for any cold drinks or as a garnish for fish dishes.

To make neat orange slices and segments

Slice an unpeeled orange horizontally. Remove the peel and pith with scissors from each slice separately. To make segments free from pith, peel the orange and remove the outer pith. Hold the orange in one hand, then, using a sharp knife in the other, cut each segment removing the flesh only, discarding the membrane and skin. Remember to carry out these processes over a bowl to catch the fruit juices.

To keep fruit pieces whole during cooking
Instead of stewing fruit in water and adding sugar to sweeten, poach it in a light sugar syrup (350 g/12 oz sugar to 600 ml/ 1 pint water). Dissolve the sugar in the water, bring to the boil, add the prepared fruit and cook gently without stirring until the fruit is tender. The colour will remain bright and the fruit will not cook to a mush. If the fruit is very sweet, reduce the proportion of sugar to water slightly.

Slicing canned pineapple rings into pieces quickly
Open the can, drain off the syrup and insert a long knife with a pointed blade into the centre down to the bottom of the can. Cut through the rings, all at once, from the centre to the outside, six to eight times according to the size of the rings.

Freezing melon balls and shells
When melons are cheap, buy large ones, cut in half to provide bowl-shaped shells and remove the seeds and take out all the flesh with a melon-baller. Freeze the balls in polythene bags for use in fruit salads. Open-freeze the shells then pack them separately to make containers for serving ice cream, sorbets or any other frozen dessert. If liked, vandyke the edges of the shells with scissors before freezing them.

How to cut melon in half with a vandyked edge
Mark the melon skin all round the centre without actually cutting it. Using a small, sharp, straight-edged knife, thrust it into the centre of the melon at an angle, just above the mark, then pull it out. Make the next cut into the centre at an opposite angle. Repeat all round the melon until you can pull the two halves apart; scoop out the seeds with a spoon. Small melons such as ogen can be served a half melon to each person. If the melon is larger, scoop out the flesh with a melon-baller and use each half as a case for fruit salad. Or, if liked, remove only the

top third making a much deeper case and trim the top to use as a lid, replacing it on top of the fruit filling at an angle.

How to make a melon basket

Cut a tiny slice off the bottom of the melon so it will stand firmly. Mark two parallel lines evenly either side of the stem end across the top and down to the centre of the melon. The distance between the two marks will depend on how wide you wish the handle to be. Mark round the centre of the melon on both sides without cutting the skin to join the two handle bases. Slice through downwards on each side of the handle and inwards round the side to remove two large chunks of skin complete with flesh and seeds. Scoop out the remaining seeds and trim the flesh away from the inner side of the handle. The centre of the melon basket can then be scooped out with a melon-baller to make a container for mixed fruit salad.

To soak and cook dried fruit easily

Place dried prunes, apricot halves, apple rings, etc., in a wide-necked vacuum flask and top up with boiling water. Seal and allow to stand overnight. The fruit will then be ready to eat.

To shred candied peel easily

Scrape off the hardened white sugar and soak the peel in boiling water for 2 minutes. Drain, and cut with a sharp knife.

Economical substitute for candied peel

If you are too busy to grate or pare the rind carefully off citrus fruits when you use them, remove it in larger pieces with a potato peeler. Snip the rind up with scissors into small pieces and stir it into a screw-topped jar half-filled with golden syrup. Keep adding more rind as available until the jar is full. After a few weeks' storage, well-drained pieces of rind from the jar can be used in cakes and puddings instead of candied peel.

To plump up glacé cherries

Put the cherries into a sieve and run very hot water through them. Shake well, then turn out to dry on soft kitchen paper. This also makes the cherries less sticky and easier to handle.

Economizing on Christmas luxury fruits

Exotic Christmas goodies such as glacé fruits and boxed dates are often sold at a reduced price after Christmas but their shelf life is limited. If over-wrapped and frozen these fruits will store for up to 12 months in perfect condition for the following festive season.

To improvise a fruit glaze with jelly

Make up a fruit jelly of the appropriate flavour using only half the quantity of water indicated on the packet. When the jelly is syrupy but not quite set, spoon it over the fruit. Do not be impatient because if the jelly is too liquid it will not mask the fruit successfully but will sink straight through into the base.

To make a quick glaze for tarts

Syrup from stewed or canned fruits can be brought to the boil and thickened with arrowroot moistened with cold water or cold syrup. Apricot jam, heated with a little water or lemon juice and sieved to form a smooth purée, or melted redcurrant jelly, can also be used to form quickly-made glazes for sweet dishes. For an even coating, they are best applied to the surface of the food with a pastry brush.

To give garden rhubarb a good colour

Cut it into pieces and place them in a pie dish. Make up a medium-heavy syrup in the proportion of 300 g/11 oz sugar to 600 ml/1 pint water. Tint the syrup pink with a few drops of red food colouring and pour over the fruit in the dish. Cook, covered, in the oven.

To prevent certain fruits from discolouring

Apples, pears, peaches and plums discolour when cut surfaces are exposed to the air. To prevent this, prepare the fruit directly into a bowl of salted water (rinse off when preparation is complete) or straight into sugar syrup. If using fruit raw, preserve the colour by brushing cut surfaces with lemon juice. This works well for the above fruits and also for avocado pears and bananas.

To prevent baked apples from bursting

1 Pare a thin strip of peel away all round the circumference of the apple.

2 After removing the core, slit the skin with a sharp pointed knife in 4 or 5 places from top to bottom.

To prevent sausages from bursting

Place them in a greased pan and cook gently from a cold start, turning frequently. Or put the sausages in cold water. just bring to the boil and immediately drain off the water, Dry on soft kitchen paper, then fry in the usual way. Sausages with a high cereal content are more likely to burst than others.

To prevent discoloration of white meat during cooking

Blanch the prepared pieces of meat by placing in a pan with cold water to cover. Bring to the boil as quickly as possible then drain and cook as required.

To tenderize liver before cooking
Place the liver in a dish and pour over milk to cover. Allow to stand in the milk for 1–2 hours, then drain and pat dry with soft kitchen paper. This method is particularly useful for ox liver and pigs' liver.

To tenderize a joint of beef before cooking
If you bulk-buy meat and after cooking one joint from a batch you discover that the meat is tough, try smearing mild mustard all over the next joint from the batch before roasting it.

To tenderize a cooked joint
If a joint is discovered to be tough after cooking, pour 2 table-spoons of brandy over it and return the joint to the oven for 15 minutes. It will then be tender, and the brandy will leave no noticeable flavour.

To tenderize frozen meats
Unwrap and place the frozen meat in a container. Make up a marinade and pour it over the meat. Cover, and allow the meat to defrost in the marinade, turning it several times. During the defrosting time the meat will gain flavour and become tender-ized by the marinade.

To keep stewed meat tender
To conserve the juices inside diced meat for stewing, toss the pieces quickly in hot fat to seal all the surfaces first. This prevents the juices from cooking out into the liquid. To save thickening the stew at the end of the cooking time, toss the diced meat in seasoned flour before frying. This conserves the juices even more thoroughly and gives the stew a richer, browner appearance.

Substitutes for expensive meats
Classic recipes such as wiener schnitzel require veal fillets. The difference in taste is hardly distinguishable if you use pork fillet, well beaten out, or thinly sliced turkey breast. Boeuf en croûte is another costly dish – try enclosing pork fillet or a large breast of turkey portion instead. If necessary, two pork

fillets or two turkey breasts can be sandwiched together with well-seasoned stuffing before the preliminary roasting to make a joint of the right size.

Making minced beef go further

If you mince the beef yourself, put in one slice of white bread to each 225 g/8 oz meat and no one will notice the difference. Here are other ways to extend minced beef.

1 Add dry breadcrumbs in the proportion of 1 part breadcrumbs to 3 parts minced meat.

2 Add rolled oats in the proportion of 1 part oats to 5 parts meat.

3 Add cooked rice in the proportion of 1 part rice to 5 parts meat.

4 Add soya granules mixed with water as directed on the packet.

To get a crisp crackling on roast pork

Make sure that the rind of the joint is scored deeply in narrow lines. Brush with oil and sprinkle with salt, then place in a cold oven. Roast in the usual way, allowing extra time depending on how long your particular oven takes to come to the required heat.

To make well-shaped patties or rissoles

If the mixture is too soft to be easily moulded into perfect rounds or cork shapes, return the mixture to the bowl, cover and chill for 30 minutes. It should then be possible to shape easily, using floured hands.

How to prevent lean meat from drying out during cooking

Either lard the meat by wrapping it in a thin layer of pork fat, beef suet or fat bacon, securing it in place with string, or lard the meat by threading part of the surface with thin strips of pork fat using a larding needle.

Carving a shoulder of lamb easily

Before cooking, place the joint on a board, hold the knuckle with one hand and insert a sharp pointed knife with the other, cutting round the bladebone as closely as possible. While the joint is in the oven, the meat will shrink away from the bone as it cooks. Before carving, insert a carving fork at the knuckle end and, using a kitchen cloth to protect your fingers, twist the bladebone until it is free, then pull it out. The partly-boned joint is easy to carve in neat slices.

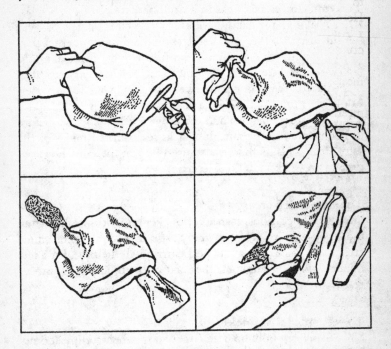

To prevent bacon from shrinking

Dust the rashers very lightly in flour on both sides before cooking. To prevent the rashers from curling up, snip them at intervals all down the fat edge after removing the rind.

Buying bacon economically

Choose bacon which has been thinly sliced. If members of your family are used to having two or three slices for a meal, they can still do so and it will cost less. Bacon pieces are a good economy buy because they often include a few slices neat enough to be used for frying and the remainder can be chopped up to use in pizza toppings, flan fillings or for any recipe which requires chopped bacon as an ingredient. Odd-pieces of fat and rind can be slowly rendered down to provide excellent fat for frying bread and crisp nutty pieces to use, finely crumbled, in soups or toppings.

To avoid excess saltiness in boiled bacon

After soaking, and before cooking, pass clean fingertips over the cut surface of the joint and test on the tongue whether they are noticeably salty. If there is no further time for soaking to remove excess salt, bring the joint to the boil in plenty of water, then discard the water and cover the joint with fresh water. Cook it in the usual way, or if it is particularly salty, add a whole potato to the pan and discard this when cooked, before it begins to disintegrate. It will have absorbed much of the salty taste. This method is also useful when there has not been time to pre-soak a joint of bacon.

To make a rich creamy gravy

For special occasions, instead of thickening juices in the pan in the usual way to make a gravy, stir in 150 ml/¼ pint single cream and place over a low heat, stirring all the time, for a few minutes without allowing the mixture to boil. Strain into a warm gravy boat.

To set aspic jelly quickly

Since aspic can only be used for coating when syrupy and not quite set, it is important to bring it to this point quickly. Use only enough boiling water to dissolve the crystals and make up to the required amount with cold water. Put the solution in a metal container then place this in a bowl of crushed ice. The aspic will reach setting point within a few minutes, so test frequently to see whether it is becoming syrupy, and when it does, remove it from the bowl of ice. If aspic sets too quickly, stand the container in a bowl of hot water to liquefy. To show off the colour of the food, leave aspic its natural colour; to coat a meat loaf, stir in sufficient meat extract to the hot aspic to colour it brown and increase the savoury flavour.

How to make a cutlet frill

Cut a strip of clean white paper 5 cm/2 in by 12.5 cm/5 in and fold it in half lengthways. Snip the folded edge at 28 mm/⅛ in intervals half-way towards the open edges. Begin winding the paper from one end spirally round a pencil as tightly as possible, and secure the end with a dab of adhesive. When dry, slip the frill off the pencil.

To keep pasta shapes separate during cooking

Add oil to the water used for cooking – 1 tablespoon for up to 225 g/8 oz pasta shapes – they will then glisten and stay separate after draining.

How to cook long pasta shapes evenly

Oil the base of the pan, fill with plenty of salted water and bring to the boil. Hold one end of a bundle of long pasta such as spaghetti or macaroni and lower the other end into the pan. As it softens, gradually coil in the remaining pasta until it is all submerged under the boiling water. Stir gently after the water has returned to the boil.

Time savers with pasta

If lightly cooked pasta is coated with oil while still hot, shapes or strands will stay separate when reheated or after freezing. Frozen pasta can be made ready for the table by turning out the pack directly into a pan of boiling water. When the water returns to the boil, the pasta is ready to serve. You can save time when preparing most layered dishes which cook the pasta together with a sauce by using raw pasta instead of cooked, but be sure that the top is layered with sauce.

How to improve sticky boiled rice

Turn the rice into a sieve or colander and pour boiling water through it. This removes traces of rice flour. Drain thoroughly and spread in a shallow ovenproof dish. Place, uncovered, in a moderate oven, or lightly covered with foil in a fairly hot oven, to dry out.

To make golden rice

Saffron stands are expensive and you may find a few strands are insufficient to colour a large quantity of cooked rice. If so, reinforce the colouring by adding a few drops of yellow food colour to the cooking water. If preferred, omit the saffron altogether and use turmeric and yellow food colouring instead.

To reheat cooked rice

Put the rice into a non-stick saucepan with a few tablespoons of water and place, covered, over a low heat. Do not stir the rice, but shake the pan occasionally until the rice has absorbed all the water and become hot and fluffy. Or, if the oven is in use, enclose the rice in a foil parcel with a knob of butter. The parcel of rice will take from 20–30 minutes to heat according to the temperature of the oven and the quantity to be heated.

Using up left-over boiled rice

Transform it into fried rice. Heat 2 teaspoons oil in a frying pan for each 100 g/4 oz cooked rice. Add the rice to the pan, stir gently to separate the grains without breaking them up, and when they are hot sprinkle in a little soy sauce and chopped spring onion. To make it more interesting, pour in 1 lightly-beaten egg and continue to cook, stirring, until the egg is just set.

To pluck poultry or game birds

Place the bird in a bowl and pour boiling water over it. Allow to stand for 2 minutes then drain. Tie the feet together with string and loop this over a strong hook or door knob. Starting with the wings and working against the direction in which the feathers grow, pull out a few at a time, jerking sharply. The strong feathers at the wing tips will need to be removed one at a time, and a pair of pliers is sometimes useful to enable you to get a good grip on them. Work up one wing towards the tail, then pluck the other wing. Start plucking the neck half-way between the head and the body. Continue plucking, again towards the tail, then turn the bird over and pluck the other side. Any small hairs that are left can be singed off over an ignited gas ring or with a lighted match or taper.

To draw poultry or game birds

Place the bird breast uppermost on a working surface. Cut through the neck half-way between the head and the body and remove the head. Push the skin of the neck back towards the body and grasp the neck inside. You will need to use soft kitchen paper or a clean cloth in order to get a good grip. Twist the neck until it becomes separated from the body and withdraw it. Insert two fingers into this flap of neck skin and loosen the crop and gizzard. Cut through the skin on one leg half-way between the foot and the first joint, and place the bird so the leg sticks out over the edge of the table and snap the bone. Pull off the foot, together with the tendons, of which there should be seven. Repeat with the other leg, then lay the bird flat with the breast uppermost and away from you. Mark a point about 5 cm/2 in up from the vent towards the breast. Make a slit here, insert two fingers of one hand with the knuckles uppermost and draw out all the intestines, including the crop and gizzard which are positioned at the neck end of the bird. Sever all these from the inside of the bird with a sharp knife and cut away the vent, leaving a large cavity. Of the giblets, keep only the neck and the liver, after carefully removing the greenish gall bladder. Do not puncture this latter organ or the liver will have a bitter flavour when cooked.

To truss poultry or game birds

Place the bird on a working surface with the legs pointing towards you and tuck the wing tips under the body. Fold the neck skin underneath. Place a long piece of string under the bird, holding the neck skin in place. Take the right-hand end of the string and bring it up along the right-hand side of the body, cross it over the cavity and loop it around the left drumstick bone. Do the same with the left-hand end of the string, looping it round the right drumstick bone. Draw both pieces of string downwards, cross them over under the parson's nose, then tie them together over the parson's nose. Trim off the ends.

Trussing poultry with a trussing needle

A neater and more professional-looking result can be achieved if you truss your bird using a special needle threaded with fine string. Place the bird on a flat surface with the breast uppermost and close the neck opening by folding the skin underneath. Have the needle ready threaded with about 1 metre/ 3 feet 3 in of string. Pass the needle through one wing joint, the carcase and out through the other wing joint, leaving an end long enough to tie hanging out. Then insert the needle through the body above the wing and out at the other side. Pull the thread taut and tie with the loose end to make a tight knot, cutting the thread close to this knot. This secures the wings close to the body. Now insert the threaded needle up through the parson's nose, leaving sufficient string to tie hanging out. Twist the string round first one drumstick, then the other, pass it down through a different hole in the parson's nose, pull the thread tight and tie firmly. Cut the thread close to this knot.

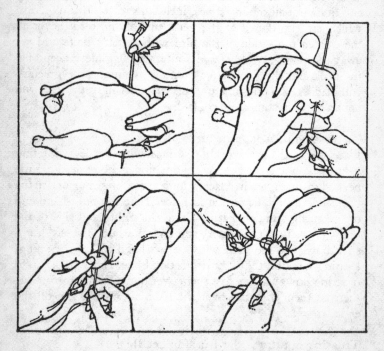

How to bone a chicken

Place the chicken, breast side downwards, on a flat surface. Cut along the backbone with a sharp knife, then, holding one side of the skin and flesh in one hand, cut the flesh away from the rib cage using a sharp knife in the other hand. Keep gathering up the flesh and skin and separate the flesh from the bones with the knife. Sever the leg bone from the body and pull it, turning the skin and flesh inside-out, then pull out the bone. Do the same with the wing bones. Continue pulling the skin and flesh and severing it from the bones until you reach the breast bone, then repeat this process with the other side of the bird. You should then be able to lift out the backbone, rib cage and breast bone in one piece. Fill boned chicken with a ham joint, pâté or stuffing, and reshape it, pushing the filling into the leg and wing bone cavities. Sew up the skin where the backbone used to be.

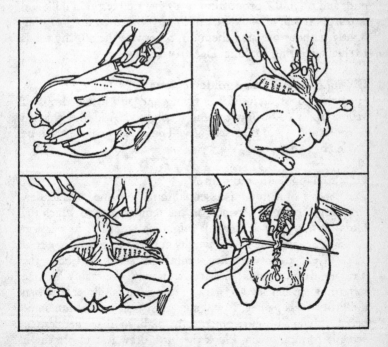

To speed up the cooking time for unstuffed poultry

If you insert a metal spoon, or two forks, into the cavity of the bird before cooking, the length of time can be reduced by about 5 minutes per 450 g/1 lb. This is because metal is a good conductor of heat.

To get a crisp coating on skinned chicken from the freezer

Soak the skinned chicken in cold water until thoroughly defrosted, then take it out and coat it all over in flour. Leave it in the flour for a few seconds, then place it on a plate and allow to stand for 30 minutes. Shallow fry in 1.5 cm/½ in hot oil in the usual way, turning once only. The coating will stop the chicken from absorbing excess oil.

To get a crisp crust on chicken or veal

Sprinkle with salt, coat in flour and dip in a mixture of egg, milk and oil in the proportion of 1 egg, 1 tablespoon milk and 1 teaspoon oil. Coat all over in dry breadcrumbs, turning lightly without pressing them on, otherwise the coating tends to shell off during cooking. Deep fry in oil.

Giving fried chicken a golden colour

Heat the oil or fat used for frying and add a few drops of yellow food colouring to tint it slightly. Add the chicken portions and fry in the usual way. The cooked chicken will be golden brown.

How to hang feathered game

The process of hanging is essential to make game birds tender. The length of time depends on the temperature in which the birds are hung, as one week might be sufficient in a warm atmosphere while ten days would not be too much in a cold place. Tie the legs together firmly with string and hang the bird up from a hook, head downwards, preferably from a rafter in a garden shed or garage, safe from family pets. When the bird smells gamey, it will suit most tastes, although some people prefer it to become really high so that the flesh is actually turning green. Pluck the bird, draw it, and prepare it for roasting in the same way as a chicken. Keep the pheasant cock bird's tail feathers to garnish the roasted bird. At this stage the prepared bird can be packed and frozen exactly as you would chicken, and is also defrosted in the same way. When cooking, always protect the breast with fat or streaky bacon to prevent it drying out.

Hanging game birds for freezing
For freezing, hang for 1 day less than usual. The bird will become more 'gamey' while defrosting. If you are pressed for time, wrap and freeze game birds without drawing or plucking them. It is a messy job when the birds are defrosted, but is actually easier than carrying out the same processes before freezing, especially the plucking.

Tenderizing game in a marinade
Game meat is often tough and you may hesitate to hang it until it smells really 'gamey'. Older birds, hare or venison all taste delicious and become tender if marinated in oil and red wine then braised with the marinade, made in the proportion of 2 parts oil to 1 part wine.

To remove the fishy taste when cooking water birds
When the bird is ready for cooking, plunge it into a large pan of boiling water for 1 minute, then drain well and pat dry with soft kitchen paper. Alternatively, pour boiling water over the bird then drain and dry. Repeat once.

To prevent scum from forming on jam
Add a knob of butter with the sugar. If some does form, avoid skimming until the jam is cooked, otherwise a considerable quantity of jam will be wasted. Most of it will have disappeared by the time the jam reaches setting point.

Pressure-cooking marmalade
Save time and trouble by pressure-cooking the pulp and then, after adding the sugar, using the open pressure cooker as a preserving pan.

To test jams, jellies and marmalades for setting point
Stir the mixture and insert a thermometer. When the tempera-

ture reaches 104°C/220°F for jam and jelly, and 106°C/222°F for marmalade, a set will be obtained when potted. To test for a set without a thermometer, remove the pan from the heat, place a little of the mixture on a cold plate and allow it to cool. Draw a fingertip through the centre and if the surface wrinkles and the mixture stays in two separate sections, setting point has been reached. Remove the pan from the heat each time you test for a set, otherwise it can overcook during those few minutes.

To get a good set when jam-making

Combine fruits with a low pectin content such as strawberries and those with a high pectin content, such as rhubarb. This is an example where the strongly flavoured berry fruit predominates; another good combination is blackberry with apple.

To pot jam easily

Have clean, warm, dry jars ready. Use a ladle, small jug or cup and fill each jar to within 1.25 cm/½ in of the top. Wipe the filled jars while still hot with a hot damp cloth, paying great attention to the inside of the tops of the jars before covering and sealing them.

To liquefy honey or preserves which have crystallized

Place the jar in a pan of warm water over low heat until all the crystals have disappeared, then stir well. Preserves often become granular if stored in a refrigerator and are better kept in a dry cupboard.

To make mincemeat go further

Add coarsely-grated cooking apple to the mincemeat before cooking in the proportion of 1 medium cooking apple to 225 g/8 oz mincemeat.

To prepare home-made spiced vinegar for pickles

Place malt vinegar and flavourings in a stainless steel, aluminium or non-stick pan in the proportion of 1 teaspoon ground nutmeg, 2.5-cm/1-in piece cinnamon stick, 50 g/2 oz whole pickling spices and 4 cloves to each generous 1 litre/2 pints malt vinegar. Bring slowly to boiling point, remove from the heat, cover and allow to stand for up to 3 hours. Strain through a very fine sieve and cool before using.

A quick method to cook dried beans
If you forget to soak dried beans overnight, use this quick method. Bring a generous 1 litre/2 pints water to the boil, add 225 g/8 oz beans, bring back to the boil and cook for 2 minutes. Remove from the heat, cover the pan and allow to stand for 1 hour, after which the beans can be used as if they had been soaked overnight.

Economy hint on buying nuts
When it is possible to buy nuts in the shell cheaply, it may be worth your time and trouble to shell them yourself as the price will still compare favourably with the price of packaged shelled nuts. Most nuts are easier to crack when in the frozen state.

Making an economy peanut butter
Liquidize 100 g/4 oz salted peanuts with half the weight of soft margarine or softened butter until the mixture is smooth enough to spread. If you prefer not to use butter, substitute 25 g/1 oz margarine and 1 tablespoon vegetable oil. Pack the peanut butter in a jar with a screw-topped lid. If a crunchy type is preferred, finely chop a few extra peanuts and stir into the blended mixture before placing in the jar. If you make a large quantity, it will probably be considerably cheaper than bought peanut butter.

How to prepare almonds for cooking
To blanch almonds, place them in a saucepan of cold water, bring slowly to the boil, then remove from the heat and drain. As soon as the nuts are cool enough, slip off the skins by pinching them between finger and thumb, then rinse the nuts in a basin of cold water. Drain again and dry by spreading out on soft kitchen paper. Use as required, or store in an airtight container. If you need to halve, shred or flake almonds, do

119

so while the nuts are still damp as they become brittle and difficult to handle when completely dry.

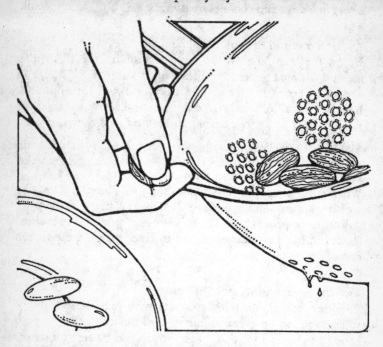

To make lump-free gravy with pan juices

Place 1 tablespoon flour and about 300 ml/½ pint cold or warm water in a screw-topped jar or airtight polythene container. Seal, and shake vigorously until blended. Add this to the meat juices in the roasting tin and stir briskly until boiling.

To make white sauce quickly and easily

Place the butter (or other fat), flour and milk in a saucepan and whisk over moderate heat until the sauce boils and thickens. Simmer for 2 minutes then add seasonings or flavourings as required.

To add gloss to white sauce

When the sauce has thickened, simmer for at least 2 minutes to ensure that the flour is cooked. If the sauce still lacks gloss, beat in a knob of butter or beat 1 egg yolk with a tablespoonful of the hot sauce. Stir this mixture into the sauce over the heat then remove the pan from the heat without allowing it to boil.

How to make a smooth cheese sauce

Remove the pan containing the sauce from the heat, add the grated cheese, and stir constantly until the cheese has melted and the sauce is smooth. If the sauce is boiled after the addition of the cheese it will become stringy.

Substituting condensed canned soups for sauces

If used undiluted, these soups are so strong and full of flavour that they are a worthy substitute for omelette and pancake fillings, and combined with cooked minced meat, they produce an instant savoury dish. They give an upgrading transformation to any stew that turns out thin, watery and disappointing.

To prevent a skin forming on sauces

When the sauce is cooked, cover the surface immediately with a layer of cling wrap or damp greaseproof paper. If the sauce is a sweet one, such as custard, sift a thin layer of icing sugar over the top and stir this into the sauce when ready to serve.

To prevent sauces thickened with egg from separating

Beat the egg or eggs in a basin, add a little of the simmering sauce to the egg and stir briskly. Pour this mixture into the sauce in the pan, stir in vigorously, then remove from the heat without allowing the sauce to boil.

To make blender mayonnaise

Break a whole egg into the goblet and add 1 tablespoon lemon juice or vinegar and seasoning to taste. Switch the blender on high and gradually pour in 150 ml/$\frac{1}{4}$ pint vegetable oil through the top aperture. The mayonnaise should form within 30 seconds.

To retrieve curdled mayonnaise

If you enjoy a piquant flavour, gradually beat the mayonnaise a little at a time into a teaspoon of mild made mustard. If not, beat it gradually into an additional egg yolk. It may be necessary to add more oil. Taste, and adjust the seasoning when the mayonnaise has the right consistency.

To make French dressing quickly

Have all the ingredients at room temperature, measure them and place them together in a screw-topped jar. Put on the lid and shake vigorously until the mixture emulsifies. Store in a sealed jar or bottle and shake each time before using.

To make a quick chocolate sauce

Combine equal quantities of cocoa and golden syrup in a saucepan and stir over gentle heat until well blended. This sauce is ideal to serve over ice-cream or plain steamed puddings.

To keep seasoned flour readily available

Combine flour, salt and pepper in the proportions of 4 tablespoons flour, 1 teaspoon salt and $\frac{1}{2}$ teaspoon pepper and keep in a flour dredger ready for coating meat for frying, or for stews and for making gravy.

Making mustard

When you make up dry mustard, add a few drops of glycerine and it will remain moist for a week without drying out and forming a skin.

Correcting a fiery curry

If the curry is made with chicken, add sufficient natural yogurt to make the flavour milder. If it is made with beef, add coconut 'milk'. Pour 300 ml/$\frac{1}{2}$ pint boiling water over 3 tablespoons desiccated coconut. Allow to stand for 30 minutes then strain as much of the liquid as is required into the curry.

To remove excess salt from soups or stews

If the cooked food tastes too salty, add a whole, peeled, raw potato and allow to cook until the potato is fairly soft but not breaking up. If necessary, add a little more unsalted liquid. Before serving, remove the potato and taste the dish again. Sometimes the potato can be kept and eaten separately so there is no need to waste anything.

To keep salt free-flowing

In a damp atmosphere, salt often becomes moist and cakes in the salt cellar. Add a few grains of rice when you fill the cellar with salt to absorb excess moisture and keep the salt running freely.

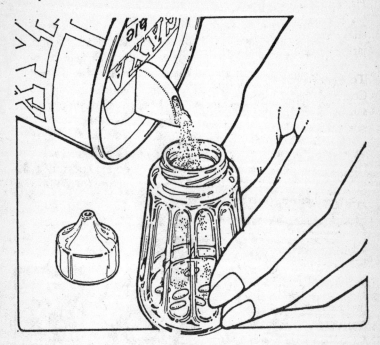

Seasoning for cold soups and sauces

When cooking sauces and soups to be served cold, slightly over-season them, as on cooling the strength tends to fade a little. Most vegetable and bean soups taste delicious served cold, enlivened with extra seasoning and a few drops of lemon juice just before serving.

To clear a consommé

Add a lightly whisked egg white and a clean egg shell during the last 30 minutes of cooking time. Strain before using. The egg white will have helped to precipitate albumen into the liquid, leaving it clear.

Adding inspiration to canned consommé

Place sufficient consommé to serve four people in a pan with 8 tablespoons of white wine, or 4 tablespoons of dry vermouth. Bring to the boil, cover and simmer for 10 minutes. Then add 1 tablespoon of dry sherry and serve at once.

Removing excess fat from soups

If there is a thick layer of fat on the surface of a hot soup or stew, drop in 4 or 5 ice cubes. Have ready a slotted draining spoon to immediately spoon them out, otherwise the cubes will begin to melt and dilute the soup. Solidified fat will have adhered to the ice cubes during the brief moment they were in the soup.

To remove garlic cloves easily from soups and stews

Peel the garlic clove and spear it with a wooden cocktail stick. Cook it on the stick with the stew then it will be easy to find and remove before you serve.

How to make economy pea soup

Fresh peas in the pod seem expensive compared with the frozen variety, but pea pods, like other vegetable skins, are extremely nutritious. Wash and cook them in plenty of lightly salted water until tender, then rub through a sieve leaving all stringy parts behind. The resulting purée makes a delicious soup. Pea pods are also good as a basis for home-made wine.

To use up left-over soup

Left-over vegetable and bean soups are exquisite served cold. They usually thicken as they cool so will require extra cold chicken stock, or milk, or cream stirred in per portion. Top with finely chopped parsley.

To serve soup without splashing

Rinse out a jug with very hot water. Transfer the soup to the jug and pour steadily into the soup plates, holding the lip of the jug close to the edge of the plate.

Making party dips from condensed soups

Almost any canned condensed soup makes a good party dip if well beaten into cream cheese in the proportion of 150 ml/ ¼ pint undiluted soup to 150 g/5 oz cream cheese. Particularly suitable soups are cream of celery, chicken, mushroom or tomato.

To cook crisp onion rings easily

Cut an onion into slices then separate it into rings. Dip in evaporated milk then in flour and deep-fry, a few at a time, in hot oil until golden brown and crisp.

To make soft fried onions

Place the sliced onion in a strong frying pan, cover it with water, salt lightly, cover the pan and cook until almost soft. Remove the lid and cook over a high heat until the water is almost evaporated. Add small knobs of butter or dripping and continue cooking, stirring frequently, until the onion browns. The onion does not frizzle up and it produces a greater volume than if fried from the raw state.

To prevent artichokes discolouring during cooking

If they are to be eaten on their own or masked in a sauce, scrub them and cut them into large pieces. Place in a pan and add 1 tablespoon lemon juice or vinegar for each 450 g/1 lb, then cover with salted water and cook until tender. Leave the artichokes in the cooking water until cool enough to handle, then drain them and slip off the skins by pinching between finger and thumb.

Slicing cooked vegetables neatly

Cooked beetroot for salads and par-boiled potatoes for frying can be neatly sliced on a wire egg slicer. The centre of the potato must be just sufficiently cooked to be easily sliced by the wires.

Slimmer's way with chipped potatoes

Buy the frozen kind, but don't deep-fry them; bake them in the oven instead. Spread them out on a baking sheet and sprinkle with salt before cooking for extra flavour.

To prevent unpleasant odours when cooking vegetables

Cauliflower, cabbage and Brussels sprouts sometimes smell most unappetizing during cooking. To prevent this, place the prepared vegetables in a saucepan, add water as required, then place a slice of toasted bread on top before putting on the lid. Discard the bread after cooking.

To cook frozen peas without water

Melt a knob of butter in a small saucepan and add seasoning and a few outside lettuce leaves which have been shredded. Add the peas, stir well, cover the pan tightly and cook over gentle heat for about 5 minutes. Check whether the peas are cooked. If not, cover the pan again and cook for a further 2 or 3 minutes. The lettuce keeps the peas moist during cooking.

To cut the baking time for jacket potatoes

Scrub the potatoes in the usual way then place in a saucepan of boiling water and cook for 5 minutes. Drain, prick all over with a fork, then bake. The potatoes will be ready to eat about 20 minutes earlier than usual. Or scrub the potatoes, cut them in half lengthways and score the cut surfaces diagonally in both directions with a sharp pointed knife to a depth of 1.5 cm/½ in. Spread with butter and bake, cut sides uppermost, until tender.

To give a glazed finish to root vegetables

Boil sliced root vegetables in the usual way until just tender, then drain well. To each 450 g/1 lb cooked vegetables, add a knob of butter and a teaspoon of sugar to the pan and sprinkle in a teaspoon of flour. Shake over moderate heat for about 2 minutes, by which time the flour will be cooked and will have formed a nice glaze with the butter and sugar.

To chop onions safely

Cut a peeled onion in half. Place the flat side of one half down on a board and hold it at the stalk end with a carving fork. Slice finely first lengthways away from the fork, then across, working up to the fork.

To use up surplus onions

Once onions begin to sprout they will soon turn bad. If you cannot use up a surplus in cooking within a few days, peel and chop them, discarding any doubtful portions, then cook in as little water as possible until soft. Either pack in small quantities in polythene bags for freezing, over-wrapping the bags to prevent the odour escaping and tainting other food, or liquidize the cooked onions and freeze in used yogurt or cream tubs which you can discard when the contents have been used. Seal with foil caps and over-wrap. Do not use ice-cube trays because the smell of onions is so difficult to dispel.

Peeling garlic or onions without tears

Drop them into a pan of boiling water, bring back to the boil and allow 5 seconds for a clove of garlic, 10 seconds for a baby onion and up to 5 minutes for a really large onion. Drain, rinse in cold water, and the papery skin will just slip off with finger pressure.

To crush garlic without a garlic press

Remove the papery skin from a clove of garlic, place it on a flat surface and sprinkle with salt. Press with the flat blade of a knife enclosed in a folded piece of foil to avoid impregnating the knife blade with the smell of garlic.

Flavouring a green salad with garlic

1 Cut a plump clove of garlic in half and rub the inside of the salad bowl with the cut surfaces of the garlic.
2 Cut the garlic clove as above, and rub it over a small crust of French bread. Toss the bread with the salad and dressing, then remove the bread.
3 Marinate the cut garlic clove in the dressing for 1 hour before serving the salad. Remove the garlic before pouring on the dressing.

To give potato salad a mild onion flavour

Either cook a peeled onion with the potato, then remove before making the salad, or cut a large onion into quarters and push them into the prepared salad. Cover and chill for at least 2 hours then remove the onion before serving.

How to keep watercress fresh

Trim off the stalk ends short, and place the bunch in a tumbler with only the stalky part in water. Put the whole thing in a polythene bag and seal the top with a twist tie. Stand the tumbler carefully in the refrigerator, open the bag and snip off sprigs as you need them. The bunch will keep fresh for one week.

To ripen green tomatoes

Wrap each tomato separately in a twist of paper and put a dozen or so together in a bag. If you have any ripe ones, put one ripe tomato in each bag. Place the bags in an airing cupboard or drawer in a warm place and take a peep after four days. Remove the tomatoes as they ripen and store them in the refrigerator. Exposing green tomatoes to light turns them bitter and pulpy and they take longer to ripen.

Slicing tomatoes easily

Use a serrated knife and slice downwards with the stem end on top, so that slices are cut with the grain of the core for sandwiches, to keep in the juices; slice with the stem end at the side, across the core, to release the juices.

To use up green tomatoes

To dispose of a surplus other than by making pickles, try frying thick slices, sprinkled on both sides with seasoned flour, in melted butter. Add a little soft brown sugar when you turn the slices. They taste as good as cooked ripe tomatoes.

Skinning frozen tomatoes

Hold a frozen tomato under running cold water with one hand and rub the skin gently with the other. It will split and slip off immediately.

Cooking frozen tomatoes successfully

Slightly thaw the tomatoes, cut in half acrossways with a finely-serrated knife, dot with butter, and grill. Or place the cut sides upwards in a frying pan with fat and fry without turning. Once fully defrosted, tomatoes tend to collapse and lose their texture.

To peel tomatoes quickly

Insert a kitchen fork at the stem end and hold the tomato close
to a gas jet, turning it gradually until the skin splits. Or put
the tomatoes in a basin, pour over sufficient boiling water to
cover and leave to stand for 1 minute. Drain off the water,
pour over cold water to cover, and peel the tomatoes, starting
with a cross-shaped split at the stem end. The boiling water
method also works well for grapes, peaches and nectarines.
Tomatoes and peaches can also be peeled quickly and easily in
a microwave oven – see page 15.

To chop fresh herbs quickly

Put a few sprigs of washed herbs, stripped from the stalks if
necessary, in a teacup. Hold the handle with one hand and snip
up the herbs with kitchen scissors with the other, gradually
turning the cup. Shake the cup occasionally to redistribute the
herbs. For a small quantity, fine chopping is achieved in less
than 1 minute.

To make a tomato water-lily

Using a sharp, pointed knife make a diagonal cut in towards the centre of the tomato at a point just above the middle. Make the second cut away from the base of this cut on the opposite diagonal to form a zig-zag. Mark out with the tip of the knife or a fine skewer where the peak of each triangular cut should come, so that they will be evenly spaced round the tomato, then complete the cutting. Pull the two halves gently apart. Use either as they are, or scoop out the seeds from the centre and fill with a parsley sprig or a few cooked peas or corn kernels, for colour contrast.

Using up mushroom stalks

When whole mushrooms are required, it is usual to trim the stalks off level with the caps and often these trimmings are thrown away. When you prepare a quantity of mushrooms, chop the stalks and sauté them lightly in butter with seasoning and herbs to taste. When cooked, cool and pack in plastic tubs covered with foil. Kept in the refrigerator for several days, or frozen, these make handy additions to stews, soups and sauces.

Making vegetable garnishes

To make a **radish rose**, trim off the root and stalk. Holding the radish by the stalk end, cut across from the root end to within 0.75 cm/¼ in of the stalk end. Cut three more times, dividing the radish into eight segments. Place the prepared radishes in iced water and leave for 30 minutes for the 'petals' to open out.

To make **celery curls**, cut celery sticks into pieces about 7.5 cm/3 in length. Keeping the centre intact, make parallel cuts about 3mm/⅛ in apart out to both ends. Leave in iced water as above. To make **onion brushes**, trim both ends and cut spring onions to a length of about 10 cm/4 in. Using a sharp knife, make a 1.5 cm/½ in cut at the bulb end of each onion. Cut 3 more times, dividing the bulb into 8 segments. Leave in iced water as above.

To make **onion fronds**, trim spring onions as above. Insert the tip of a sharp pointed knife into the onion about 5 cm/2 in from the stalk end and pull upwards through the green part. Do this several times then leave in iced water as above.

Using vegetable stock
Water used for cooking any vegetables provides a mild-flavoured stock which is excellent in gravies, soups or used instead of boiling water to make up a packet of stuffing mix. It can also be used to make up instant potato to increase the flavour and nutritive value.

Index

Dates, to cut up 19
Deep-frying 92–3
Defrosting freezers 14
Dips from condensed soups 125
Dividers for freezing, improvised 29
Draining oily foods 93
Drawer lining, cheap 53
Drawing poultry or game birds 113
Dried beans, to cook quickly 119
Dried fruit, plumping in microwave 15 ; soaking and cooking 104
Duck fat, to use up 93
Dumplings, to make fluffy 79

Earthenware cooking dishes, to maintain 23
Earthenware teapot, to clean 49
Egg boxes, uses for 42
Egg poacher, improvised 28
Egg timer, extra uses for 18
Eggs. *See also* Meringues, Omelettes, Pancakes
  Boiling a cracked 90
  Economy egg wash 90
  Enriching sauces with yolks 88
  Freshness testing 92
  Frying in microwave 16
  Poaching in microwave 15
  Preventing discoloured hard-boiled whites 92
  Scrambled 90 ; in microwave 16
  Storing in frozen state 88
  Using left-over whites 90
  Using left-over yolks 89
  Ways to separate 88
  Whisking whites successfully 87
Evaporated milk, to whip 83

Fahrenheit, converting to Celsius 13
Fat-free diet 40
Filter, improvised, for coffee pot 28
Filtering liquids 26
Fish:
  Buying 94
  Cooking large whole 96
  Court bouillon and stock 96
  Filleting 94
  Frying 95
  Poaching 95
  Removing scales 95
  Skinning 95
Fish brick, to clean 23
Flans:
  Baking a meringue case 91
  Filling with frozen fruit 55
  Preventing sogginess in pastry 76
Flour, seasoned 122
Flour dredger, to improvise 27
Foil, to re-use 46
Fondues, cheese, hints for 85
Freezer:
  Calculating storage capacity 59
  Cleaning 13
  Defrosting 14
  Improvised containers 29
  Improvised trays for open-freezing 29
  Saving space for open-freezing 58
  Using melted frost from 42
  Working out running costs 59
Freezer mitt, magnetic, to make 13
Freezer pack labels, improvised 29
Freezer tape, to keep ready 58
French dressing, quick 122
Fritters, to make light 91
Fruit. *See also* Citrus fruit, Dried fruit *and* Apple etc.
  Choosing 36
  Filling a flan with frozen 55
  Freezing, for wine making 54
  Glaze from jelly 105
  Keeping pieces whole during cooking 103
  Preventing discolouring 105
  Quick topping and tailing 101
  Removing traces of pesticide 37
  Using up canned syrup 47
  Using up juice 81
Frying foods, hints for 92–3

Myra Street

MIXER AND BLENDER COOKBOOK

Carefree cooking at the flick of a switch. Use these indispensable kitchen aids to save you time, toil and trouble. From soups and sauces to soufflés and meringues —whatever you use your mixer and blender for, you can be sure of perfect results every time.

Myra Street was born in Scotland and trained at the Glasgow College of Domestic Science and at Atholl Crescent in Edinburgh. After qualifying, she moved to London to start her career as a demonstrator for a food manufacturer. Eighteen months abroad provided the opportunity to gain experience of continental food habits. She then moved into the editorial world as Cookery Editor to The Hamlyn Group. Although she is now teaching Home Economics at Harrow College, she still finds time to write cookery books as well as a regular monthly feature in *Homes and Gardens*.

Prices and postage and packing rates shown below were correct at the time of going to press.

FICTION

All prices shown are exclusive of postage and packing.

GENERAL FICTION

☐ THE AFFAIR OF NINA B.	Simmel	£1.20
☐ H.M.S. BOUNTY	John Maxwell	£1.00
☐ TY-SHAN BAY	R. T. Aundrews	95p
☐ A SEA CHANGE	Lois Gould	80p
☐ THE PLAYERS	Gary Brandner	95p
☐ MR. FITTON'S COMMISSION	Showell Styles	85p
☐ CRASH LANDING	Mark Regan	95p
☐ SUMMER LIGHTNING	Judith Richards	£1.00
☐ THE HALO JUMP	Alistair Hamilton	£1.00
☐ SUMMERBLOOD	Anne Rudeen	£1.25
☐ PLACE OF THE DAWN	Gordon Taylor	90p
☐ EARTHLY POSSESSIONS	Anne Tyler	95p
☐ THE MASTER MECHANIC	I. G. Broat	£1.50
☐ THE MEXICAN PROPOSITION (Western)	Matt Chisholm	75p

CRIME/THRILLER

☐ THE TREMOR OF FORGERY	Patricia Highsmith	80p
☐ STRAIGHT	Steve Knickmeyer	80p
☐ THE COOL COTTONTAIL	John Ball	80p
☐ JOHNNY GET YOUR GUN	John Ball	85p
☐ CONFESS, FLETCH	Gregory Mcdonald	90p
☐ THE TRIPOLI DOCUMENTS	Henry Kane	95p
☐ THE EXECUTION	Oliver Crawford	90p
☐ TIME BOMB	James D. Atwater	90p
☐ THE SPECIALIST	Jasper Smith	85p
☐ KILLFACTOR FIVE	Peter Maxwell	85p
☐ ROUGH DEAL	Walter Winward	85p
☐ THE SONORA MUTATION	Albert J. Elias	85p
☐ THE RANSOM COMMANDO	James Grant	95p
☐ THE DESPERATE HOURS	Joseph Hayes	90p
☐ THE MOLE	Dan Sherman	95p

(H13A:10–12:79)

NON-FICTION

☐ THE HAMLYN BOOK OF CROSSWORDS 1		60p
☐ THE HAMLYN BOOK OF CROSSWORDS 2		60p
☐ THE HAMLYN BOOK OF CROSSWORDS 3		60p
☐ THE HAMLYN BOOK OF CROSSWORDS 4		60p
☐ THE HAMLYN FAMILY GAMES BOOK	Gyles Brandreth	75p
☐ LONELY WARRIOR (War)	Victor Houart	85p
☐ BLACK ANGELS (War)	Rupert Butler	£1.00
☐ THE SUNDAY TELEGRAPH PATIO GARDENING BOOK	Robert Pearson	80p
☐ THE COMPLETE TRAVELLER	Joan Bakewell	£1.50
☐ RESTORING OLD JUNK	Michèle Brown	75p
☐ FAT IS A FEMINIST ISSUE	Susie Orbach	85p
☐ AMAZING MAZES 1	Michael Lye	75p
☐ GUIDE TO THE CHANNEL ISLANDS	Janice Anderson and Edmund Swinglehurst	90p
☐ THE STRESS FACTOR	Donald Norfolk	90p
☒ WOMAN × TWO	Mary Kenny	90p
☐ THE HAMLYN BOOK OF BRAINTEASERS AND MINDBENDERS	Ben Hamilton	85p
☐ THE HAMLYN CARTOON COLLECTION 2		70p
☐ WORLD WAR 3	edited by Shelford Bidwell	£1.25
☐ THE HAMLYN BOOK OF AMAZING INFORMATION		80p
☐ IN PRAISE OF YOUNGER MEN	Sandy Fawkes	85p
☐ THE HAMLYN FAMILY QUIZ BOOK		85p
☐ BONEY M	John Shearlaw and David Brown	90p
☐ KISS	John Swenson	90p
☐ CARING FOR CATS AND KITTENS	John Montgomery	95p
☐ PUDDINGS AND DESSERTS (500 Recipes)	Monica Mawson	85p
☐ THE HAMLYN PRESSURE COOKBOOK	Jane Todd	85p
☐ HINTS FOR MODERN COOKS	Audrey Ellis	£1.00

COOKERY

☐ MIXER AND BLENDER COOKBOOK	Myra Street	80p
☐ HOME BAKED BREADS AND CAKES	Mary Norwak	75p
☐ EASY ICING	Marguerite Patten	85p
☐ HOME MADE COUNTRY WINES		40p
☐ COMPREHENSIVE GUIDE TO DEEP FREEZING		40p
☐ COUNTRY FARE	Doreen Fulleylove	80p
☐ HOME PRESERVING AND BOTTLING	Gladys Mann	80p
☐ WINE MAKING AT HOME	Francis Pinnegar	80p

All these books are available at your local bookshop or newsagent, or can be ordered direct from the publisher. Just tick the titles you want and fill in the form below.

NAME...

ADDRESS ....

....

Write to Hamlyn Paperbacks Cash Sales, PO Box 11, Falmouth, Cornwall TR10 9EN
Please enclose remittance to the value of the cover price plus:

UK: 25p for the first book plus 10p per copy for each additional book ordered to a maximum charge of £1.05.

BFPO and EIRE: 25p for the first book plus 10p per copy for the next 8 books, thereafter 4p per book.

OVERSEAS: 40p for the first book and 12p for each additional book.

Whilst every effort is made to keep prices low it is sometimes necessary to increase cover prices and also postage and packing rates at short notice. Hamlyn Paperbacks reserve the right to show new retail prices on covers which may differ from those previously advertised in the text or elsewhere.

(H14:10–12:79)